TREATING PATIENTS
WITH MEMORIES OF ABUSE

TREATING PATIENTS WITH MEMORIES OF ABUSE: LEGAL RISK MANAGEMENT

SAMUEL J. KNAPP, EdD
AND
LEON VandeCREEK, PhD

AMERICAN PSYCHOLOGICAL ASSOCIATION
WASHINGTON, DC

Published by
American Psychological Association
750 First Street, NE
Washington, DC 20002

Copies may be ordered from
American Psychological Association
APA Order Department
P.O. Box 92984
Washington, DC 20090-2984

In the UK and Europe, copies may be ordered from
American Psychological Association
3 Henrietta Street
Covent Garden, London
WC2E 8LU England

Typeset in Palatino by EPS Group Inc., Easton, MD

Printer: Data Reproductions Corporation, Auburn Hills, MI
Cover Designer: Minker Design, Bethesda, MD
Technical / Production Editor: Catherine R. Worth

Library of Congress Cataloging-in-Publication Data

Knapp, Samuel.
    Treating patients with memories of abuse : legal risk management / Samuel J. Knapp, Leon VandeCreek.
        p.   cm.
    Includes bibliographical references and index.
    ISBN 1-55798-441-7 (acid-free paper)
    1. Psychotherapists—Malpractice—United States. 2. Adult child sexual abuse victims—United States. 3. Child sexual abuse—Treatment. I. VandeCreek, Leon. II. Title.
    KF2910.P753K59   1997
    616.85′8369—dc21   97-15987
                                                                          CIP

British Library Cataloguing-in-Publication Data
A CIP record is available from the British Library

Printed in the United States of America
First edition

To Janemarie Heesen Knapp
and
Barbara VandeCreek

Contents

Page

PREFACE..xi

Chapter 1: Scope of the Problem 1
    Threats to Psychotherapists.........................2
    Placing the Threats Into Perspective................3

Chapter 2: Liability Risks of Psychotherapists.............7
    Types of Complaints.................................8
    Litigation Arising From the Recovery of
        Memories of Childhood Abuse..................15
    Determining Professional Standards.................29

Chapter 3: Scientific Basis of Memory.....................31
    Fundamental Information About Memory.........32
    Status of Scientific Knowledge About Memory
        of Traumas....................................34

Chapter 4: Risk Management: Diagnose Carefully........47
    Standards for Identifying Past Abuse..............49
    Overidentification of Past Abuse 50
    An Alternative View of Diagnosis 56
    Child Abuse and Later Psychopathology 57
    Patients Who Request Help in Recovering
        Memories 60
    Special Problems in Diagnosing Dissociative
        Identity Disorder..............................61
    The Psychology of Clinical Judgment.............62

Chapter 5: Risk Management: Conduct Good
Psychotherapy..67
    Maintaining Proper Boundaries With Patients 68
    Choosing the Right Intervention...................74
    Outcomes With Memory Retrieval Techniques 77

Cautions When Using Memory Retrieval
  Techniques 82
Other Treatment Procedures...................... 85
Obtain Informed Consent (Patient Participation) .. 88
Show Concern for Family Relationships........... 92
Building a Healthy Skepticism 100

Chapter 6: Documentation, Consultation, and
Supervision... 107
The Use of Routine Documentation 108
Using Consultation and Supervision Properly.... 112

Chapter 7: Public Policy Considerations................ 119
Shortcomings of the Mental Health Consumers
  Protection Act................................. 120
More Adequate Controls Over Psychotherapy.... 125

Chapter 8: Conclusion................................. 131
Competent Psychotherapy Is Safe
  Psychotherapy.................................. 132
Psychotherapy Should Be Based
  on Behavioral Science 132
Greater Public Protections Are Needed........... 133

References 135

Appendix A: Risk Management Checklist.............. 145

Appendix B: Statements That May Reflect
Substandard Practices 147

Appendix C: Sample Informed Consent Form........... 149

Appendix D: Signals That May Suggest Distorted
Memories.. 151

Appendix E: Statement by the American Psychiatric
Association 153

Appendix F: Final Conclusions of the APA Working
   Group on Investigation of Memories
   of Childhood Abuse................................. 159

Appendix G: Statement by the British Psychological
   Society... 173

Appendix H: The Australian Psychological Society
   Limited Code of Professional Conduct and
   Guidelines Relating to Recovered Memories 177

AUTHOR INDEX.. 185

SUBJECT INDEX 189

ABOUT THE AUTHORS 197

Preface

Our society has made strides in recent decades in acknowledging the reality of child abuse, attempting to prevent it, and providing treatment and justice to its victims. These gains may be compromised by the recent controversy over the "false memory" debate. According to some advocates, a large number of well-meaning but misguided or incompetent psychotherapists are misdiagnosing patients and inaccurately attributing their problems to child abuse. They further allege that these psychotherapists use iatrogenic treatment techniques that unwittingly implant false memories of abuse. This controversy has been accompanied by an increase in lawsuits by disgruntled patients, or by their relatives, against psychotherapists for allegedly implanting false memories.

As a result of this backlash, many conscientious and competent psychotherapists are reportedly afraid to treat patients who claim to have been abused as children. Although there are some examples of substandard practices, we believe that the vast majority of psychologists treat patients within acceptable standards of care and in accordance with the APA *Ethical Principles for Psychologists and Code of Conduct* (1992). The likelihood of being sued always entails a certain amount of randomness. However, we also believe that competent psychologists need not avoid patients who have been, or think they have been, abused as children.

By reviewing the litigation surrounding the false memory debate, we hope to provide psychologists with an extra measure of judiciously applied "defensive practice." This review identifies certain treatment procedures that courts have found to fall outside the gambit of acceptable professional practice. We also identify ethical violations commonly alleged in the treatment of patients who litigate.

In addition, the book may be especially helpful for psychology educators and supervisors. Many of their students and supervisees may be unfamiliar with the APA *Ethical Prin-*

ciples of Psychologists and Code of Conduct (1992), have unscientific notions about the creation and retrieval of memories, or be uninformed about acceptable professional standards in the diagnosis and treatment of patients who suspect they have been abused.

Finally, we want to acknowledge to our readers that we refer to patients in this book with the pronouns *she* and *her* more often than *he* and *him*. Our choice of pronouns reflects our observations that the majority of patients about whom we are writing are women. We do not intend to minimize thereby the seriousness of sexual abuse for men and the distress adult men experience when they have been abused as children.

1

Scope of the Problem

Psychotherapists who treat adult survivors of childhood abuse provide a valuable public service. Their patients may be among the most needy, vulnerable, and traumatized of all psychotherapy patients. Psychotherapy may play a crucial role in facilitating the recovery of these survivors. The work of psychotherapists who treat adult survivors of childhood abuse is especially commendable given the way that society has historically denied or neglected its reality. Because of varying definitions and other methodological problems inherent in measuring abuse, the estimated frequency of abuse in the United States varies from 2% to 10% of all children (Berger & Thompson, 1995). However, even if the percentage of children abused is only 2% of the population, the total number is still quite large.

Most adult survivors recall the fact, and many relevant details, of their childhood abuse. According to the reports of two task forces (Alpert et al., 1996; British Psychological Society, 1995) some survivors do forget and then later recall memories of past abuse. A survey by Pope and Tabachnick (1995) found that the phenomenon of recovering memories of abuse during psychotherapy occurs in almost 1% of the patients seen by psychologists (2,452 patients recovered memories of childhood abuse out of 273,785 patients seen). Although 1% of patients is a small percentage, it still represents a large number of people.

In another study, Williams (1994) found that 38% of women who had hospital records of being sexually abused as children did not recall the abuse when interviewed 17 years later (and 12% could not recall any abusive situation). Feldman-Summers and Pope (1994) found that 40% of psychologists who alleged that they had been abused as children reported having a period of forgetting the abuse. About half of the respondents claimed they had external corroboration of the abuse. The most frequently reported factor related to later recall was psychotherapy, although other events triggered memories as well. Elliott and Briere (1995) reported similar statistics from a stratified random sample of the general population. Of those who reported a history of sexual abuse, 42% described some period of time when their memory had been absent or less complete than it was at the time of data collection.

These and other studies of survivors who had lost and later recalled past abuse have methodological limitations (see comments by Lindsay & Read, 1995) and probably overestimate the frequency of lost and recovered events. Nevertheless, few doubt that some people do lose and later recall past abuse, particularly if it was an isolated event or occurred at an early age.

Threats to Psychotherapists

Unfortunately, some psychotherapists are reportedly reluctant to treat adult survivors of child abuse because they fear litigation from former patients, or the parents of their patients, who may claim that the psychotherapists implanted false memories (Fox, 1995). Techniques commonly associated with the allegations of implanted memories include age regression, body work (the recovery of memories that are allegedly stored within body tissues), trance writing, narcoanalysis (amobarbital sodium), or the improper use of hypnosis, guided imagery, journaling, and dream interpretation. In other treatment approaches vulnerable to litigation, adult children "divorce" themselves from their "toxic" families of origin or the psychotherapists *reparent* (relate to the patient as if the patient were a child) their patients.

Lawsuits against psychotherapists who are treating survivors of childhood sexual and physical abuse have increased rapidly in the last several years. Butler (1995) reported that 150 recanters have initiated lawsuits against former therapists, and *repressed memory* (lost and then later recovered memory) complaints accounted for 16% of all claims filed in 1994 against the mental health professionals insured by the American Professional Agency (Repressed Memory Claims, 1995). Three years previously, the American Professional Agency had received no claims arising from lost memory cases. Caudill (1995) noted that the repressed memory lawsuits could bankrupt the professional liability system if they continued unabated. Caudill's brief on one defendant claimed that the therapist was being sued as "part of a concerted action undertaken by members of the False Memory Syndrome [FMS] Foundation to manufacture litigation against therapists" (1994, p. 6). Although we know of no proof for this allegation, it does demonstrate the degree of contention among professionals working in this area.

One advocacy group has promoted the Mental Health Consumers Protection Act, which would place very strict controls over the practice of psychotherapy (Barden, 1994). Others have asked Congress to restrict reimbursement for psychotherapy, unless the procedures have demonstrated scientific support (Barden et al., 1994). A critique of these legislative remedies is presented in chapter 7 on public policy. Finally, the *FMS Foundation Newsletter* makes legal information available to former patients and parents who are interested in suing psychotherapists.

Placing the Threats Into Perspective

Psychotherapists must face the problem of how to treat patients who may recall forgotten memories of abuse without engaging in practices that could implant false memories of abuse. The issue has serious implications. On the one hand, psychotherapists should not feel threatened into ignoring a serious childhood event that may have profound implications for their patient's current functioning. Ignoring that potentially important event may weaken the effectiveness of psychotherapy, and patients may suffer for years or even the rest of their lives because they could not get an effective treatment for their mental disorder.

On the other hand, psychotherapists need to be prudent about concluding that childhood abuse did occur unless patients have clear memories or can obtain supporting evidence. Few events could be more upsetting to a parent, disruptive to a family, or ultimately damaging to the patient than unfounded accusations of abuse. Goldstein and Farmer (1993, 1994) and Pendergast (1995) have described the anguish suffered by family members who found themselves accused of abusing their child or children. Sometimes parents were completely taken aback by the allegations that occurred 20, 30, or even 40 years after the alleged abuse. There have even been reports of deathbed confrontations. Families have sometimes become split into warring factions as siblings and other relatives take sides in the dispute. Parents have had to spend large amounts of money defending themselves against these suits.

From the standpoint of psychotherapists, the liability risks are far less when treating patients who always knew that they were abused as children, who retrieved the memories spontaneously, or who have valid corroborating evidence of the abuse. In these situations, a reasonable person would not be likely to accuse the psychotherapist of implanting false memories. "If we are talking about a clear, specific account [of childhood abuse] from an older child, teenager, or adult, we can agree that most are probably true" (Berliner & Loftus, 1992, p. 572). Liability risks are slightly higher when the patient retrieves memories through talk therapy. However, even then psychotherapists can greatly reduce their liability risks if they document the content and nature of their treatment sessions and the processes by which the patient recovered the memories. Liability risks are highest when psychotherapists use techniques with little or no scientific support (such as trance work, body memory work, or age-regression) to retrieve memories purported to be accurate. As described thoroughly in this volume (see chapter 5), there are reasons to believe that these techniques may actually impede the process of discovering accurate memories and may create inaccurate memories of past events. Informing patients of the limitations and possible negative side effects of these techniques would probably reduce liability risks substantially. In addition the potential for liability always increases when psychotherapists engage in boundary violations such as developing social relationships with patients or when they encourage their patients to confront or sue the alleged perpetrators.

Psychotherapists may believe that the recent increase in lawsuits is the result of guilty parents denying past events or unstable patients lashing out against innocent psychotherapists. This is probably true in some situations, but it does not appear to explain all the lawsuits. According to victim advocate and trauma expert John Briere (1992),

> Although part of the outcry regarding incompetent therapists who "implant" false memories of abuse is undoubtedly specious, it is also true that some very bad "therapy" in this area is being done by individuals with insufficient training, experience, and/or psychological stability. (p. 292)

This book describes how psychotherapists who treat patients with lost and recovered memories of childhood abuse can reduce their risk of being charged with an ethics complaint or being sued for malpractice. Psychotherapists can reduce their risks by following professional ethics codes as well as by maintaining appropriate therapeutic boundaries, diagnosing patients carefully, using sound clinical techniques based on scientific and professional knowledge, obtaining informed consent for treatments (especially those that are not scientifically proven), showing concern for the patients' future relationships with their families, documenting the diagnosis and treatment adequately, and using consultation and supervision properly. We believe that psychotherapists who treat adult survivors of childhood abuse according to the principles and safeguards described in this volume will be able to discharge their professional responsibilities with competence and will reduce the risk of being charged with negligence or unethical behavior to an acceptable level.

The essential risk management principles are reiterated in summary points in Appendix A. A set of statements or beliefs by psychotherapists considered to be high risk is presented in Appendix B. A sample informed consent form is contained in Appendix C. A summary of clinical signals that may suggest distorted memories is found in Appendix D, and statements of professional associations on the issue of lost and recovered memories are found in Appendix E through H.

2

Liability Risks of
Psychotherapists

The reasons patients decide to sue their psychotherapists or to file ethics charges against them vary and depend on the unique characteristics of the patients and their treatment experience. Although we do not wish to minimize the complexity of motives in filing complaints against psychotherapists, it is commonly found that such complaints are accompanied by ill feelings toward the psychotherapist (Simon, 1992). If patients suspect that their psychotherapists did not respect them or placed other concerns above helping them, then patients can become militant about seeking redress for any perceived ethical or professional error, however trivial. Obviously, ill feelings toward psychotherapists and negative outcomes in therapy, such as failure to improve or worsening symptoms, are intertwined. Patients who have ill feelings toward their psychotherapists are less likely to have benefited from treatment, even if the treatment offered is appropriate and has strong scientific or professional support for its clinical efficacy. Conversely, patients who fail to get better (or get worse) may develop ill feelings toward their psychotherapists, even if their psychotherapists treated them with respect and used appropriate diagnostic and treatment techniques.

This chapter reviews the types of litigation that can arise from working with survivors of childhood abuse. That litigation could include children suing their parents, however, the bulk of this chapter will focus on litigation in which the

7

psychotherapist is a defendant. "Third party suits," in which a nonpatient (such as a parent) alleges injuries, will be reviewed, in addition to suits in which the patients allege harm. In reviewing this literature, we have relied heavily on the writings of authors who are often highly critical of professional psychology and other mental health professions. It is not our intent to comment on the accuracy of every report. Instead, our goal is to alert psychologists to the types of complaints that could be made against them. First, however, we review the specific types of complaints, for example, ethics charges, malpractice suits, and so forth, that could be made against psychologists working in this area of practice.

Types of Complaints

Patients can seek redress against psychotherapists through several channels, including ethics committees, state licensing boards, or the courts. When a psychotherapist is employed by an institution, patients may also file a complaint with the psychotherapist's employer or an institutional review board. Other laws, such as those prohibiting insurance fraud or mandating reporting of suspected child abuse, may also be invoked against psychotherapists. Boundary violations such as sexual relations with patients are also subject to criminal prosecution in some states. Of course, psychotherapy supervisors are legally responsible for the actions of their supervisees regardless of the disciplinary venue being considered (see review by Harrar, VandeCreek, & Knapp, 1990).

Patients often seek redress through several mechanisms simultaneously. The ethics committee of one state psychological association found that 19 out of 27 patients who filed complaints had also filed complaints with the state licensing board or the Ethics Office of the American Psychological Association, or both (Knapp, 1994). It is possible that additional patients filed complaints with the licensing boards or other ethics committees after they finished their efforts to seek redress through the state ethics committee. The author [S.K.] knows of one case where the aggrieved patient initiated six disciplinary actions against one psychologist for the same incident, including filing a malpractice suit and disciplinary complaints before two state licensing boards, the ethics committees of two state psychological associations, and the Ethics Office of the American Psychological Association.

Ethics Committees and Licensing Boards

Complaints before ethics committees or state licensing boards require only the allegation that the ethics code of the professional association or the state licensing board was violated. The patient need not prove personal harm. Consequently, patients who proved that a psychotherapist had, for example, violated professional boundaries and entered into a dual relationship would have grounds for an ethics complaint even if the patients could not prove that they were harmed by the behavior. However, those patients typically would not have grounds for a malpractice suit, unless they could prove that they suffered actual harm.

Complaints against psychotherapists before ethics committees or state licensing boards are easy to file. Any aggrieved person can complete the necessary forms, and ethics committees do not require complainants to have an attorney. If the attorneys for the licensing board believe that the complaint has merit, then they will handle the complaint, sparing the plaintiff the litigation costs. However, the burdens of ethics complaints on the providers are increased by the fact that licensing boards and ethics committees may have different rules, procedures, time-lines, and elements of due process.

A professional association's ethics committee can issue letters of reprimand or censure, or, in extreme cases, revoke the membership of the practitioner. Very often ethics committees also require supervision or education that attempts to rehabilitate the professional. At first consideration, the removal of a practitioner from a professional association or a disciplinary letter may seem minor to the aggrieved patient; however, the very existence of a sanction from a professional association may label the practitioner as a high risk for malpractice insurance or for managed care panels, which almost always ask the applicants if they have been investigated or disciplined by an ethics committee or a licensing board.

State licensing boards have typically adopted codes of ethics identical or similar to those used by professional associations, although these boards have more authority to regulate psychotherapists. Because of their authority as licensing boards, they can mandate supervision or further education as a condition of continued licensure. If circumstances warrant, they can also restrict or revoke the practitioner's authority to practice. As with ethics committees, even "minor" sanctions such as a reprimand or censure can make it difficult for the practitioner to purchase malpractice insurance or be accepted on a managed care panel.

Malpractice Suits

The legal requirements of a malpractice suit can be summarized by four D's: the psychotherapist owed a *Duty* to the patient, the psychotherapist *Deviated* from acceptable professional standards, and that deviation *Directly Damaged* the patient. Malpractice suits differ from ethics complaints in several ways. In a malpractice suit, the person suing must be a patient of the psychotherapist, thus creating the special duty between the psychotherapist and patient (see the following section for unusual exceptions to this rule). Once this special, or fiduciary, relationship is established, a malpractice suit can be considered. A narrow, but long-standing series of cases have recognized an exception to this rule when a patient poses an imminent threat of harm to an identifiable third party (this "duty to protect" rule will also be discussed later in the chapter).

To be vulnerable in a malpractice lawsuit, the behavior of the psychotherapist must have deviated from the acceptable standards of the profession. Typically the courts will rely on expert witnesses from the same profession or field as the treating psychotherapist to advise them on the established standard of care. Some memory retrieval techniques (e.g., age regression and body work) lack widespread acceptance, and therefore it could be difficult for a plaintiff to find a mental health expert who could convince a court that the techniques were part of the acceptable practice of psychotherapy.

In determining appropriate standards of care, judges will assume that a deviation from a professional code of conduct constitutes a deviation from acceptable standards of care. This fact is particularly relevant to the discussion of litigation regarding the treatment of adult survivors of childhood abuse, because many patients allege ethical violations (especially boundary violations) in their complaints. For patients to sue successfully, they must show that the deviation from professional standards directly caused them harm. A blatant breach of confidentiality, for example, would, by itself, be grounds for a charge before an ethics committee or licensing board where it is not necessary to prove harm. However, it would not be grounds for a successful malpractice suit unless the patient could prove that he or she was directly harmed by the breach.

The standard of care is not to be thought of as the level of care of the average among all practitioners ranging from the worst to the best, but rather as the reasonable average level of care among ordinarily good practitioners. Similarly, the utmost degree of skill attainable in the profession is not required. Nor are professionals required to exercise their best skills at all times. Professionals are not expected to be perfect nor to be functioning at peak performance constantly. In addition, some states allow for comparative negligence, whereby patients can be held to share in the harm they suffered. For example, a patient who failed to take medication as prescribed could be held to have some responsibility for the negative outcome. In such instances, the patient might be held accountable for a portion of the financial settlement assessed by the court.

Respected minority rule. The standard of care is particularly difficult to establish in mental health practice as there are many different schools of thought about most areas of practice. Judges and juries are not expected to understand all of the theories about human behavior that practitioners are expected to understand. Rather, courts will rely on experts to instruct them on the standards of practice within a profession. Some courts will allow the *respected minority rule,* whereby the behavior of psychotherapists will be evaluated according to their particular *school of thought* as long as there are a respected number of practitioners in that school of thought. This school of thought must be recognized and be in good standing in the profession and have established rules of practice. Nontraditional treatment procedures (those treatments lacking wide professional or scientific endorsement) may be especially vulnerable to malpractice charges unless patients have been fully informed about the experimental nature of the procedures and have given their informed consent to the procedures. According to precedents within medicine, this has been used, for example, to have oral surgeons testify as to the techniques of other oral surgeons, instead of allowing the testimony of dentists who may be trained in different techniques to treat the same malady.

The respected minority rule could conceivably be applied to require testimony by psychotherapists who use similar memory recovery techniques. However, the definitions of what constitutes a school of thought within psychotherapy are less clear, and the court could define school of thought very narrowly and may not include as wide a variety of opinions as the defendant psychotherapist might have wanted. This is particularly true with recovered memory techniques, some of which do not have adequate scientific or professional support to warrant belonging to a respected or accepted school of thought. According to Alpert (1996),

> The search for buried memories is not promoted by professional programs in psychology or mainstream professional literature on the treatment of adult survivors.... There is no training program or mainstream literature that presents memory retrieval to the exclusion of other therapeutic tasks as the treatment goal or that promulgates the utilization of techniques that are suggestive. (p. 7)

Specialists. Psychotherapists who market themselves to the public as specialists through advertisements, business cards, or other means will be held to a higher standard of care than "general practitioner" psychotherapists. Specialists will be expected to possess more knowledge and use more sophisticated techniques for treating the disorder than non-specialist psychotherapists. A psychotherapist who claims to be a specialist in hypnosis, for example, would be held to a higher standard of care in its use than the nonspecialist psychotherapist, even if that psychotherapist occasionally used hypnosis. The specialist psychotherapist who uses hypnosis to recover memories of past abuse would have other specialists in hypnosis testify as to what every specialist in hypnosis should know and do. In contrast, the average "general practitioner" psychotherapist who just happens to have used hypnosis will be held to a lower standard of care. For example, in one of the cases reviewed in this chapter, *Ramona v. Ramona* (Marine & Caudill, 1994), it was alleged that the treating social worker had mistakenly identified herself as an expert in treating anorexia and bulimia, thus allowing her conduct to be evaluated according to the standards of experts in those fields (Cruz-Lat, 1994a).

Proving harm. Traditionally, complainants in malpractice suits have had difficulty proving that the psychotherapy harmed them, because the damage assessment depended on the self-report of persons who have something to gain by falsifying or exaggerating their symptoms. The difficulty of proving harm can be understood as a problem of satisfying the "but for" causation requirement. That is, the harm alleged by the patient would not have occurred but for the defendant's negligence. Psychological harm is not impossible to prove, however. According to the *FMS Foundation Newsletter* (Suits Against Abusive Therapists Settled, 1995), in one case settled out of court, the complainant relied on the results of her initial MMPI (Minnesota Multiphasic Personality Inventory; which were well within normal limits) and those of an MMPI taken after treatment (some scores were now outside of normal limits). An expert witness opined that the dramatic deterioration in MMPI scores could be attributed to a serious trauma, such as substandard psychotherapy. Generally, courts have been more willing to accept the validity of the complaint when the damage can be assessed objectively such as through a suicide attempt, job loss, or disrupted family relationship. Patients have also had difficulty proving the direct link between their harm and the behavior of the psychotherapists. That burden may be easier to meet when the psychotherapists assumed responsibility for retrieving lost memories of childhood abuse, and the patients disrupted their family relationships based on that belief.

Defamation

Defamation has become a source of complaints by third parties against psychotherapists. Although specific states and provinces vary in their definitions of defamation, generally defamation includes a false communication that "tends to injure 'reputation' in the popular sense; to diminish the esteem, respect, goodwill, or confidence in which the complainant is held, or to excite adverse, derogatory, or unpleasant feelings or opinions against him" (Prosser, 1971, p. 739). Defamation includes the twin torts of libel (communications that are written or broadcast over the radio or TV) and slander (other oral communications). Most cases of defamation to date have occurred because of the unauthorized disclosure of information, although defamation could also occur because of gratuitous comments made from authorized disclosures as well (see review by Simon, 1992).

The application of the defamation tort to psychotherapists would depend on the circumstances of the case and the exact wording of the law in the jurisdiction. Although truth is a defense against charges of defamation, the truth of statements involving memories of abuse is difficult to prove. Nonetheless, charges of defamation could occur when a psychotherapist comments publicly that a patient was abused. If public comment is necessary for the treatment of the patient (such as in a letter summarizing treatment to a future psychotherapist or in notes shared with third-party payers), then the psychotherapist should make it clear in the letter that the information about abuse is based on the patient's report.

Other Avenues of Redress

Many psychotherapists work for institutions that have review boards, or they work under the direct supervision of other mental health professionals. Often their employment contracts include a requirement that they follow the ethical standards of their profession. Although the standards may be identical to those used by ethics committees and licensing boards, the institution or employer provides aggrieved patients with another venue to seek a redress of grievances. Psychotherapists are also regulated by various other laws such as those prohibiting insurance fraud or mandating reports of suspected child abuse. Although these laws may have little to do with treating adult survivors of childhood abuse, angry parents or former patients may invoke them in an effort to punish psychotherapists.

Litigation Arising From the Recovery of Memories of Childhood Abuse

The recent litigation concerning memories of childhood abuse can be placed into three categories of complaints: adult children against their parents, parents against the psychotherapists of their adult children, and former patients against psychotherapists. Although the litigation between adult children and their parents does not involve psychotherapists directly, the strength of the lawsuit often relies on the patient's belief in the ability of the psychotherapeutic techniques to recover accurate memories. During the course of this litigation, the methods of the psychotherapist may come under scrutiny. Furthermore, the anger engendered by the lawsuit may precipitate a suit against the psychotherapist by the parents (or even the former patient).

Lawsuits have even been initiated against the authors Bass and Davis for writing the book *Courage to Heal* (1988, 1994), which was alleged to be responsible for implanting false memories in its readers. These suits were dismissed with prejudice because the First Amendment to the Constitution of the United States of America protects free speech and because the authors had no fiduciary relationship to the readers and no responsibility for a standard of care. We consider these lawsuits to be frivolous and will not review them further. Nonetheless, the fact that the suits were initiated attests to the high risk of litigation when working in this area.

Adult Survivors Against Their Parents

Some adults who believe that they were abused as children will initiate a civil suit against their parents, guardians, or other adults for the abuse they endured. Poole, Lindsay, Memon, and Bull (1995) reported that almost 6% of the adult patients who recovered lost memories of childhood abuse while in psychotherapy initiated lawsuits against their abuser. Data from the False Memory Syndrome Foundation reveal that about 7% of the family members who contacted the organization were being sued (Legal Actions Against Parents, 1994).

Victims of childhood abuse often have difficulty pursuing a prosecution because the abuse itself may create such fear and trauma that the victims have difficulty asserting themselves against the perpetrators until long after the statute of limitations has passed. The legal issues become more complicated when the victims allege that lost or repressed memories of abuse did not return to their consciousness until many years later. A federal court, in *Johnson v. Johnson* (1988), classified suits against perpetrators into two types. In the first type, the complainants claimed that they had always remembered the abuse, but did not become aware that the abuse had caused their psychological problems until many years later. In the second type of cases, the plaintiffs claimed that they had no recollection of the abuse until many years later.

The discovery rule. A major impedient for these lawsuits is that the usual statute of limitations is two years or, in the case of minors, two years after they reach majority age. The statute of limitations typically expires before the adult is free enough from the effects of the abuse to initiate the suit. A number of states have, however, recently extended the length of time to age 30 before suits can be barred. A detailed state-by-state review of these laws can be found in Pope and Brown (1996).

Another impediment to a lawsuit occurs when the adult has allegedly repressed or lost the memory of the abuse. The acceptance of a lawsuit when a memory is lost or repressed often depends on the court's interpretation of the *discovery rule* that permits plaintiffs to extend (*toll*) the statute of limitations if they did not discover the harm (or a reasonable person would not have discovered the harm) until the statute of limitations had expired. The statute of limitations may be tolled if the plaintiff, or a reasonably prudent person, did not discover the wrongful acts within a specified period of time (usually two years). This discovery rule is an exception to the general rule that the statute of limitations begins to run for a specified number of years (usually two years) as soon as the right to initiate the suit begins.

The classic medical example of the discovery rule is of a patient who had surgery years ago. The surgeon left a sponge in the patient's body, but the patient did not feel pain until more than two years later. A reasonably prudent person would not have suspected the harm until many years later when his or her abdomen began to hurt. Some adult survivors of childhood abuse who have sued after the two year statute of limitations has expired have argued that the statute of limitations should be waived because the memories of the abuse were lost or repressed and did not come to light until many years later.

Cases of both types require the modification of the discovery rule. In Type I cases, which involve remembered abuse that was not conceptualized as wrongful or tortious until recently, courts have almost uniformly refused to extend the discovery rule, despite the fact that the patient might have always had the memories or even had corroborating evidence of the abuse. In Type II cases, which involve a recent recall of abuse that was once lost from memory, courts have differed in their interpretation of the discovery rule. Some have been generous in tolling the statute of limitations, whereas others have been very strict and have not allowed extensions based on lost or repressed memories. Several states have seen legislation introduced that would require courts to extend the discovery rule in cases of lost and then recovered or repressed memories (Clevenger, 1991–1992).

Judicial acceptance of recovered memory therapy. An argument commonly found in these cases is that the nature of the abusive event was so traumatic that the victims forced the abuse experience out of their conscious awareness. The patients do not, it is argued, become aware of precipitating traumatic events until they encounter an incidental environmental stimulus that triggers the recall of the memory or they enter psychotherapy with a mental health professional who helps them recover the memory.

Some of the suits rely on the accuracy of hypnosis or other memory recovery techniques to help patients retrieve memory of lost abuse. The judicial system has had a long history of dealing with hypnosis, especially when used to recover the memories of witnesses to violent crimes. Most courts view hypnotism with skepticism. Some refuse to accept hypnotically refreshed memories at all; others accept hypnotically refreshed memories only if certain stringent safeguards have been in place (Scheflin & Shapiro, 1989).

Although several courts have allowed complainants to sue on the basis of lost and recovered (repressed) memories, we anticipate that successful suits based on repressed memories will be less common. Over the years defense attorneys have acquired greater sophistication in obtaining expert witnesses who are willing to testify that the accuracy of memory retrieval techniques has not yet been proven sufficiently to justify a judicial determination of guilt. As one legal commentator has stated, "repressed memory research ... remains largely speculative and anecdotal, and, because it has yet to be adequately tested, no firm empirical conclusion can be drawn about the phenomenon at this time" (Faigman, 1995, p. 961).

In *State of New Hampshire v. Hungerford* and *State of New Hampshire v. Morahan* (1995), the Superior Court of New Hampshire considered cases in which the complainants alleged abuse based on memories recovered during psychotherapy. Judge Groff concisely summarized the issues surrounding the recovered memory debate and concluded that "based on the existing scientific evidence, the concept of 'repressed memory' is not generally accepted in the field of psychology, and is not in that sense scientifically reliable" (p. 3). The Judge was careful to state that his decision did not impugn psychotherapy in general nor did it preclude the possibility that the phenomenon of repressed memory might be validated in the future. The *Hungerford* case was a criminal case in which the standard of proof was "beyond a reasonable doubt." Civil cases have lower standards of proof (usually "clear and convincing" or "preponderance of evidence") that increase the likelihood of finding in favor of the alleged victim.

Parents Against Psychotherapists

Some parents have initiated lawsuits against the psychotherapists who treated their adult children. Often their suits are precipitated when patients file suits against their parents for abuse based on lost and recovered memories or after patients confront their family members with these memories. Ordinarily a legal duty exists only between a therapist and his or her patient, and the psychotherapist owes no legal duty to any outside party such as the patient's parents. An exception to this general rule has been the development of a narrowly defined duty to protect in which the psychotherapist, while treating a potentially dangerous patient (the *Tarasoff* doctrine; *Tarasoff v. The Regents of the University of California et al.*, 1976), has a legal duty of care toward an identifiable victim in imminent danger of substantial physical harm (VandeCreek & Knapp, 1993). Some aggrieved parents have argued that this duty of psychotherapists to third parties should extend to them as well.

Third-party suits with minor children. The rule against suits by third parties has seen some erosion as it applies to the treatment of minor children. It is not clear whether the courts in the cases discussed here would have reached the same conclusion if the children had been adults. Courts have been split as to whether to grant parents legal standing to institute a lawsuit against the therapists who are treating their minor children. In *Bird v. W.C.W.* (1994), for example, the Texas Supreme Court denied such standing. In this case, a therapist submitted a report of suspected child abuse against a parent living out of state, based on the child's and mother's statements. The out-of-state parent sued the psychotherapist. The court noted that state law requires psychotherapists to act to protect children of abuse and that allowing the suit to stand would contradict the intention of the child protective services law. It stated that it might allow a third-party suit under a different set of circumstances, however. Similarly, an Alabama court denied the standing of a parent to sue a psychiatrist who allegedly misdiagnosed childhood sexual abuse ("Alabama Supreme Court Rejects," 1995).

Standing for parents to sue their minor children's psychotherapists was granted in *Montoya v. Bebensee* (1988) and *Wilkinson v. Balsam* (1995). In both of these cases, the psychotherapists reported child abuse on the part of one of the parents. In *Montoya*, the court noted that a good faith reporting of child abuse was protected by Colorado's child abuse reporting law; however, it allowed the father to pursue a suit on the basis of a bad faith report. It also ruled that the father had standing to sue the therapist on the basis of her other actions, such as counseling the mother to deny the father visitation rights. Similarly, in *Wilkinson v. Balsam* (1995), the father sued on the basis of negligent psychotherapy, although the filing of the actual report of abuse was protected by the child abuse reporting law.

Third-party suits with adult children. A more direct controversy concerns the ability of third parties to sue on behalf of adult children. Except in one isolated case, courts have not recognized a duty to the parents that gives rise to a claim for relief, although courts have allowed suits to proceed on other grounds.

Cases against psychotherapists. Cases against psychotherapists by parents were unheard of several years ago. Traditionally, parents do not have a fiduciary relationship with the psychotherapist of their adult child, and therefore lack an essential ingredient that would allow them to sue the psychotherapist for malpractice. Nevertheless, we will review five recent cases in which parents have been allowed to sue psychotherapists. In one case, the child was a co-complainant in the case. The second case was based on a unique ruling in California that allowed nonpatients to sue health care providers under unusual circumstances, and the other cases involved lawsuits based on grounds other than malpractice.

The "Althaus case" was atypical because the parents joined with the former patient in suing the psychotherapists ("Girl Recants," 1994). In this case an adolescent girl made increasingly bizarre and incredible accusations against her parents, including claims of satanic ritualistic activities. She was removed from her home by child protective services, although the alleged abuse was never substantiated. The girl later recanted her stories and filed a suit, along with her parents, against her treating psychiatrist, among others.

Ramona v. Ramona (Marine & Caudill, 1994) was a unique California case in which a parent was given standing to sue the psychotherapists of his adult daughter on the grounds of negligence. The father, who was also invited to several psychotherapy sessions with his daughter for the purpose of a confrontation, argued that his direct and personal contact with the psychotherapist gave him standing to sue. Although the court did not accept that argument, it allowed the suit to proceed by relying on a California precedent that allows third parties limited status to sue when they are harmed by the behavior of a health professional (Schneider, 1994).

The father in *Ramona* alleged that the psychotherapists had implanted false memories of sexual abuse in his daughter. Although the daughter testified on behalf of her psychotherapists, the court ruled in favor of the father and awarded him $500,000 in damages. The victory was a mixed blessing, however, because the award did not cover his legal costs and the court also found contributory negligence on the part of Mr. Ramona. That is, the jury believed that the actions of Mr. Ramona contributed, to some extent, to the deterioration of his family relationship (Marine & Caudill, 1994).

Even if parents do not have legal standing to sue on the

basis of malpractice, they can sue on other grounds. In *Sullivan v. Cheshier* (1994) parents were allowed standing to sue the psychotherapist of their adult child for an intentional tort in which he allegedly caused family members to become estranged. The legal problems of the psychotherapist were increased because he was not licensed, but still implied that he was a psychologist. The information sheet given to his patients read, in part, "Although Dr. Cheshier is a member of the American Psychological Association, he has chosen not to be registered as a clinical psychologist" (*Sullivan v. Cheshier*, 1994, p. 657). The court noted that such an announcement might have violated the Illinois licensing law for psychologists.

A federal court applying Pennsylvania law allowed parents to sue the therapists of their adult daughter for breach of contract and slander (*Tuman v. Genesis*, 1995). During psychotherapy, the counselors allegedly convinced the daughter that she had repressed memories that her father impregnated her, subsequently killed the baby in a satanic ritual, and had killed her twin brother. Finally, it was alleged that the defendants had solicited money from their other patients to hide the daughter from her parents' cult that was allegedly intent on harming her. The daughter has assumed a new identity and moved out of Pennsylvania.

Although contract law is not typically applied to psychotherapist–patient relationships, the unique circumstances in the *Tuman* case allowed courts to apply it there. In *Tuman*, the parents agreed to the instructions of the therapists in the Genesis counseling center by paying for treatment on a session by session basis, and detaching themselves from their daughter for two years. The explicit relationship between the parents and the psychotherapists, which is atypical among professional relationships, gave support for the theory that contract law should apply. Furthermore, the *Tuman* court allowed the parents to sue for slander. The court noted that the daughter made statements alleging incest and murder on the part of her parents to her group therapy members. The court also allowed the parents to charge that their daughter acted as the counselors' mouthpiece by acting on the memories that the counselors implanted. However, it should be noted that the *Tuman* case only established the grounds on which a suit could be filed. The actual liability of the counselors in this case was not established.

A Texas court found a psychiatrist liable for slander for telling members of the patient's family about the alleged abuse of his patient (*Khatian v. Jones*, 1994). The facts under which the disclosure were made were especially problematic. The allegations of abuse occurred while the patient was under the influence of sodium amytal, the treating psychiatrist stated in court that he doubted the accuracy of the statements even before he told other family members, and the patient had recanted her allegations before the meeting with the other family members. Nevertheless, the psychiatrist presented the allegations as if they were fact and caused great disruption in the family. The court opined that the presentation of the finding as if it were fact (instead of an allegation) constituted slander.

Likely future directions. It is unlikely that third-party suits will become common against psychotherapists of adult children. The traditional negligence standards would not apply because no duty exists between the psychotherapist and the parent of the patient. The breach of contract suit, which was permitted in the *Tuman* case, was allowed because of the highly unusual circumstances under which the patient received treatment. Defamation, however, may become a more common source of complaints against psychotherapists, especially if family confrontations are encouraged.

Former patients against psychotherapists. The psychotherapist–patient relationship gives rise to a professional duty that is one of the grounds necessary for a malpractice suit. As noted previously, the other requirements are that the psychotherapist deviated from acceptable standards of treatment and that deviation directly resulted in damage to the patient. In the discussion on patient litigation against psychotherapists, we have relied heavily on the newsletter of the False Memory Syndrome Foundation and from books and articles written by their sympathizers. Our reliance on these sources does not mean that we believe that all the allegations are true (see Pope, 1996, for a critique of the reliability of allegations by the False Memory Syndrome Foundation). Nevertheless, we believe that psychologists can best protect themselves against allegations of substandard practice if they know the nature of past allegations that have been made against their colleagues.

Allegations have typically included charges that the psychotherapists failed to adhere to acceptable standards of care in their attempts to help patients. As part of their treatment they may have retrieved lost memories through techniques that do not have demonstrated scientific usefulness or through the misapplication of otherwise acceptable techniques. Often other ethical violations unrelated to the lost memories have been identified.

Typically patients have claimed that harm occurred to them in the form of a worsened psychological state or in impaired family relationships. The False Memory Syndrome Foundation (1995) has stated that faulty psychotherapy can create a false memory syndrome that they define as

> a condition in which a person's identity and relationships are centered around the memory of a traumatic experience which is objectively false but the person strongly believes it to be true. It has a devastating effect on the victim and typically produces a continuing dependency on the therapeutic program that created the syndrome. FMS proceeds to destroy the psychological well-being of the primary victim and the integrity of the family, and creates secondary victims falsely accused of vile acts of incest and abuse. (p. 2)

Although the sufferings of aggrieved former patients may be real, there is insufficient scientific evidence to merit the creation of a discrete diagnostic category of false memory syndrome at this time. Successful allegations of negligence would have to be based on findings other than the development of a false memory syndrome.

The sources of information about recanters (patients who claimed to have been abused and who then recanted the allegations) come from published cases, reports of cases settled out of court, and published narratives about their therapy experiences.

Published cases. We have obtained the judicial opinions in two cases dealing with recanters, both involving psychiatrists. As with other malpractice suits, courts will typically rely on the testimony of other psychotherapists to determine if the accused psychotherapist deviated from acceptable professional standards (although some courts have established standards to protect the public in the absence of professional standards; see *Helling v. Carey*, 1974). In *Joyce-Couch v. DeSilva* (1991), for example, experts testified that the sodium amytal treatments given to the patient were unnecessary and harmful. The facts in *Joyce-Couch v. DeSilva* were particularly egregious, and liability would probably have been found even if controversial memories of past abuse had not been involved. According to the published opinion of the case, DeSilva gave his patient 141 injections of sodium pentothal (10 times more than was needed, according to one expert). Furthermore, the court wrote that the psychiatrist "gave [the] patient no feedback and conducted no therapy, that he did not reveal [the] cause of [the] patient's problem to her, despite knowledge that [the] uncertainty caused her severe distress, and that he made improper sexual suggestions" (p. 287).

In *Hamanne v. Humenansky* (1995) a psychiatrist had allegedly told the patient "that she 'must have been' repeatedly sexually abused by her father, mother, uncle, grandfather, grandmother, and possibly other family members" (p. 3). It was also alleged that "under the regimen of constant threats, pressure, coercive group influence, powerful mind influencing drugs and hypnosis" (p. 5) the patient gradually began to believe the allegations of abuse. The case also involved serious allegations of multiple boundary violations including the therapist's discussion of her own serious emotional problems and failed marriages and requests that the patient perform office chores and move the therapist's furniture and files.

Unpublished cases. In the "Althaus" case briefly noted previously, a girl joined with her parents in suing the psychiatrist who, they claimed, failed to challenge or confront her stories of childhood abuse. The bizarre stories of sexual abuse and satanic worship included allegations that her grandmother flew around the room on a broom ("Girl Recants," 1994).

Several other cases have been settled out of court. For these cases, we have only isolated news reports, some of them reprinted in the *FMS Foundation Newsletter*, of the outcomes and the reasoning behind the different settlements. Published summaries of some of these suits provide some indication of the legal risks that could ensue from the use of memory retrieval techniques. This review of unpublished cases is not intended to be comprehensive. Instead, we intend to illustrate the types of allegations that have been made against psychotherapists.

In one case a patient alleged, among other charges, that the use of hypnosis to retrieve past memories of abuse resulted in a deterioration of her condition. An expert noted that the patient had a normal MMPI profile on entering therapy, but that her MMPI profile showed extreme mental deterioration and was consistent with the theory that the therapy she had undergone was traumatic ("Suits Against Abusive Therapists Settled," 1995). In another case the patient alleged that she was misdiagnosed as having multiple personality disorder and was convinced that her family had engaged in ritualistic torture, rape, and human sacrifice ("Suits Against Abusive Therapists Settled," 1995). In a third case the patient was reportedly told by her therapist that she was involved in satanic ritualistic abuse as a child and was convinced to sue her parents. Therapy consisted of being reparented by the husband and wife therapy team. The therapists allegedly encouraged the patient to call them "mom and dad" and to terminate any relationship with her biological parents ("Couple Brings Suit Over Malpractice in New Hampshire," 1995). In a final case, the allegation was made that a psychologist had inaccurately diagnosed a patient as having multiple personality disorder and had implanted false memories of abuse ("Malpractice Lawsuit Against Therapist Settled," 1995).

Narratives of recanters. The self-reported stories of recanters provide evidence of some of the actions that could precipitate lawsuits against psychotherapists. Some have alleged harmful boundary crossings, such as a patient promoting a workshop for her psychotherapist, a psychotherapist attending a party at a patient's house (Goldstein & Farmer, 1993), or a psychotherapist inviting a patient over for coffee and taking her for rides in the country (Pendergast, 1995). Other alleged boundary violations, reported by the False Memory Syndrome Foundation, have been more subtle and have included prohibiting an adult child from receiving letters from her parents ("Parents Tell Us," 1993), forbidding patients from talking to family members (Loftus & Ketcham, 1994), and pressuring patients to write angry letters to their parents (Goldstein & Farmer, 1993).

Recanters have also described psychotherapists who appeared to focus more on the identification of childhood sexual abuse than on treating the patient's presenting problem. Private investigators hired by disgruntled parents have posed as patients and have reported on the apparent exclusive preoccupation of some psychotherapists with childhood sexual abuse (Loftus, 1995). The accusations of recanters have often been combined with allegations that the psychotherapists attempted to make the former patient excessively dependent on the psychotherapists or a group therapy "family," and refused to change treatment plans despite substantial deterioration in the overall functioning of the patients (Loftus & Ketcham, 1994).

Reports also suggest that memories of abuse have been implanted through the alleged misapplication of hypnotherapy as a method to determine the accuracy of past events, and through the interpretation of body memories (the theory that physical pains and discomforts are indicators of past abuse), coercive group therapy, or trance writing (the theory that historical truth can be determined by going into a trance and writing whatever comes to mind; Goldstein & Farmer, 1993; Nelson & Simpson, 1994; "Suits Against Abusive Therapists Settled," 1995). Pendergast (1995) alleges that at least one report of childhood sexual abuse arose from communications made through facilitated communication (a procedure used with autistic children whereby the child guides the hand of an adult facilitator on a typewriter and directs the words that are typed). Some recanters have reported that they always had memories of being abused as children, but claimed that their therapists persuaded them to expand the number of abusers or the frequency of the abuse (Wylie, 1993).

A review of the recanter literature showed that there are frequent allegations of violations of ethical standards that are not necessarily tied to the allegations of implanting false memories of past abuse. Some recanters have alleged that they were discharged from hospitals prematurely, were allowed to have their insurance benefits run out without concern for extended treatment, or were dropped abruptly from treatment without a referral once they lost their ability to pay full fees for sessions (Pendergast, 1995). Another patient claimed that a hospital surreptitiously paid her insurance premiums while she was in the hospital to ensure that her inpatient treatment would be covered ("Suits Against Abusive Therapists Settled," 1995). Others allege they were given referrals to incompetent practitioners or high pressure "survivor groups" (Goldstein & Farmer, 1993).

One of the authors [S.K.] knows of a patient whose unlicensed therapist "visited" her in the hospital and encouraged her to leave against medical advice and to discontinue the medication prescribed by her psychiatrist. "They do not understand you like I do," the therapist allegedly said. The unlicensed therapist insisted that the patient had a multiple personality disorder and not a major depression as claimed by the hospital psychiatrist and psychologist. In another case, according to the *FMS Foundation Newsletter*, a family member stated that a counselor told her sister with schizophrenia that "psychiatry was a conspiracy of the 'patriarchy' and that its purpose was to take power away from women," and that all the symptoms of her alleged schizophrenia "were caused by a person's mind trying to blot out memories of sexual abuse" ("My Sister's Story," 1993, p. 8).

Surveys of recanters by Nelson and Simpson (1994) and Lief and Fetkewicz (1995) have produced results that are consistent with the anecdotal reports. Recanters reported that they recovered the memory of abuse through suggestive techniques by psychotherapists or group therapy members. They often reported that hypnosis, guided visualizations, age regression, or other techniques were used to help them regain their memories. We can neither confirm nor refute the accuracy of the accusations above, and it should be noted that many of these allegations were made against unlicensed or uncredentialed professionals, self-help groups, and lay therapists. However, these accusations would, if true, represent breaches in the fiduciary relationships to which psychotherapists are held. These reports are our best source of the nature of the accusations that could be made against psychotherapists in current or future malpractice cases.

Determining Professional Standards

As noted in chapter 1, psychotherapists can greatly minimize their legal risks by taking basic precautions when treating patients who recover lost memories of childhood abuse and by applying the same attitudes and behaviors that lead to quality patient care in general (and deter against malpractice suits). Effective treatment and good risk management includes following professional ethics codes carefully, developing an accurate diagnosis based on a collaborative relationship with patients, maintaining proper psychotherapist/patient boundaries, selecting empirically or professionally derived intervention techniques, obtaining informed consent from patients especially when using unproved techniques, and showing concern for the patients' long-term relationships with their families of origin. As much as possible, the use of treatment techniques surrounding lost memories should be consistent with a scientific understanding of the process of human memory. Consultation in difficult cases and careful documentation are also indicated.

All psychotherapists are vulnerable to being sued by their patients although the level of risk is typically low. In the previous discussion, we have reviewed the general principles of malpractice law and the types of litigation that have arisen from working with survivors of childhood abuse. The following discussion is based on our review of the legal cases related to lost memories, legal precedents from cases in related areas, and our review of the professional literature on the treatment of adults with lost memories of child abuse. As noted earlier, the determination of acceptable standards of professional conduct in a malpractice suit will come from experts who can describe acceptable standards of practice. However, in the area of treating adult survivors of childhood abuse, there are disagreements about the appropriate standard of care. The major areas of controversy are (a) the degree to which psychotherapy methods are consistent with a scientific understanding of memory formation and retrieval, (b) methods of diagnosis, and (c) treatment features that include maintaining appropriate boundaries, using memory retrieval techniques, obtaining informed consent, and showing concern for the family relationship. These areas of controversy are admittedly overlapping. For example, some psychotherapists may use memory retrieval techniques (memory work) as a diagnostic tool as well as a component of treatment. Also, the essential elements of diagnosis and treatment are derived, in part, from differing interpretations of the nature of memory and memory retrieval. As will be described in detail in chapter 3, the differences in treatment perspectives have substantial implications for the quality of treatment provided to adult patients suspected of being survivors of childhood abuse and for the exposure of psychotherapists to charges of negligence.

3

Scientific Basis of Memory

Psychotherapists who diagnose and treat patients with re-awakened memories of past traumas should select treatments that are consistent with what psychological science knows about memory creation and reconstruction. If the conduct of the psychotherapist were to be questioned in court, expert witnesses would be found to testify as to the scientific underpinnings of the procedures of the psychotherapist. Some of the diagnostic procedures and treatment techniques that place psychologists at a high risk of being sued are based on theories of memory that have become outdated by recent research.

This chapter will provide a brief review of the scientific basis of memory, especially as it relates to the loss or recovery of past memories of abuse. Psychologists who understand the current theories of memory acquisition and recovery will appreciate the complexity of the issues involved when it comes to the treatment of patients for whom past memories are a therapeutic issue. We believe that psychologists who understand the memory processes will be reluctant to promise patients that they have the ability to reconstruct historically accurate memories. Psychotherapists with this understanding will also be reluctant to use diagnostic or treatment techniques that are claimed to be able to uncover accurate memories but that lack an empirical or professional foundation. Psychologists who understand memory will recognize that memory retrieval practices can increase the likelihood that memories of past events will be distorted. The scientific knowledge about memory does suggest, however, that instances of spontaneous memory recovery should not be automatically discounted.

Fundamental Information About Memory

Memory is the way that information and personal recollections are stored and retrieved. It is an internal record of the lives and experiences of each person. That internal record is not always accurate, however. Information may be inaccurately encoded, or not encoded at all, it may fade over time, or be distorted in the retrieval process. Memory cannot always be trusted as the true representation of past events.

Penfield's Interpretation of Memory

Some people mistakenly believe that memory works like a video recorder and accurately records all the events that have occurred during their lives. According to this popular theory, people should be able to retrieve all the experiences of their lives if they are only given the appropriate retrieval cues. As a consequence, some people believe that hypnotic age-regression, trance writing, or other techniques will elicit accurate memories of past events. They assume that the memories of the past abuse exist somewhere within the mind, and that the appropriate cue will facilitate their retrieval.

This conception of memory is not accurate. Its roots may go back to the mistaken conclusions developed by the renowned brain surgeon, Wilder Penfield (1891–1976). During the 1930s, before anticonvulsive drugs were available, Penfield tried to stop the convulsions of epileptic patients by removing the portion of the brain where the epileptic focus occurred. Penfield knew that seizures were preceded by internal sensations (auras) such as a sense of fear or dread, a sense that objects are turning bright, or the onset of certain odors. Penfield identified the aura areas by touching the tip of an electrode to various parts of the brain and noting the impact on the patient's behavior. Stimulation of the auditory cortex produced buzzing sounds; stimulation of the motor cortex produced movement, and so forth. Because the brain itself has no pain receptors, only local anesthesia had to be used and the patient could be conscious during the procedure. Thus, patients could report their subjective experiences, and disruptions in their speech could be noted.

During these probings some patients frequently reported flashbacks to forgotten events. When Penfield removed the electrical stimulation the "memories" disappeared, and patients were not able to report these experiences during normal recall. The flashbacks, which had a dream-like quality to them, were often observations of other people doing things. One woman had a memory of being born. Another woman remembered being in a lumberyard where she believed she had never been. At other times, the patients reported feelings of familiarity or déjà vu. (To epileptic patients, the déjà vu feeling is sometimes a sign of an oncoming seizure.) Penfield concluded, "It is evident that the brain of every man contains an unchanging ganglionic record of successive experience ... [it is] a permanent record of the stream of consciousness," which includes "all those things of which the individual was once aware" (as cited in Hintzman, 1978, p. 301).

Problems With Penfield's Interpretation

Penfield's interpretation has several serious problems. To begin with, the memory retrieval experiences were not common. Of 530 patients who went through this procedure, only 40 had such flashbacks. In addition, these experiences were never independently verified and may not have ever actually occurred. Penfield only had the patient's perception that it was a long lost memory (and sometimes they could confirm that it was not an accurate flashback). For example, as noted, one patient remembered being at a specific lumberyard, although she asserted that she had never visited that lumberyard. Furthermore, even if Penfield is correct that some memories are permanently stored, it does not prove that all memories are permanently stored. Finally, the electrical stimulation of the brain may never duplicate the natural processes of neural stimulation. Because of these and other problems, memory researchers have discounted Penfield's interpretation of memory.

Status of Scientific Knowledge About Memory of Traumas

Penfield's interpretation that an event experienced is accurately recorded in memory forever and can be retrieved if only the proper stimulus is provided is not supported by recent evidence. The human brain does not necessarily place all sensory perceptions into its long-term memory. That is, it is possible to see an event, hear words or music, or taste and smell something and not have those sensory messages recorded in the brain. Also, current research notes that the nature of the events recorded may be altered by the circumstances under which recall occurs. The circumstantial factors influencing memory recall will be explored in more detail later in this chapter.

Despite all that is known about memory, cognitive scientists and some trauma clinicians differ in their conclusions about memories for traumas. The cognitive scientists and clinicians on the APA Working Group on Investigation of Childhood Memories of Abuse (Alpert et al., 1996) agreed that memories can be inaccurate, that past memories of traumatic events may be lost from memory, and that false memories of abuse may be implanted. However, the psychologists disagreed on the extent to which memories of abuse are inaccurate, are lost from memory, or can be artificially created.

Part of the disagreement occurs because of the different methodologies cognitive scientists and trauma clinicians use. As can be seen in Table 1, cognitive scientists have used primarily laboratory experiments that measure cognitive variables of daily or contrived events (such as watching a movie of a simulated automobile accident). Trauma clinicians pri-

Table 1

*Comparison of Experimental and Trauma-Based
Theories of Memory*

	Cognitive Scientists	Trauma Practitioners
Topics of Study	Daily events Contrived events	Traumas
Methodology	Laboratory experi- ments	Case histories
Dependent Variables	Cognitions	Emotions, behaviors, and/or cognitions
Major Limitations	Questionable applica- tions to real world events and trauma	Lack of scientific rigor
Major Findings		
Frequency and Du- ration of Event	Reinforces memory	May cause memory loss
Impact of Time	Leads to memory decay	Memory comes and goes over time

marily use case studies that look at affective, behavioral, and cognitive variables associated with particular traumas. Trauma clinicians have few empirical studies to bolster their position, whereas questions remain concerning the extent to which the cognitive scientists' laboratory experiments on typical memory apply to real world traumas.

Cognitive scientists and trauma clinicians have reached differing conclusions about the nature of the type of memories that they study. Cognitive scientists find that several factors influence recall, especially the duration, frequency, and salience of an event. According to Ornstein, Ceci, and Loftus (1996):

The research literature suggests several basic factors that have the potential to affect the strength of traces in memory: the amount of exposure to a particular event (both in terms of the length of exposure and the number of repetitions), the age of the individual, and the salience of the event (with highly salient experiences surviving longer than less salient ones). (p. 155)

In addition, memories tend to fade over time. Ornstein, Ceci, and Loftus (1996) wrote "without reinstating events or experiences (e.g., through rehearsal, prompts, or visualizations), the strength of a memory trace decreases over time" (p. 156).

In contrast to the cognitive scientists, trauma clinicians claim that repeated and prolonged abuse may produce dissociation or selective memory loss in some patients. According to Alpert, Brown, and Courtois (1996):

Trauma is, by definition, so overwhelming that it is difficult to face and to integrate psychologically. Because of this, defensive strategies for management of this overwhelming material are needed and include dissociation and numbing that, in turn, can interfere with memory processes. (p. 52)

Some trauma clinicians believe that at a certain level of high saliency the likelihood of memory loss actually increases. As noted by Alpert, Brown, and Courtois, "Memory loss is common in this type of [long-standing or repeated] trauma" (p. 56).

Despite the areas of disagreement noted above, most cognitive scientists and trauma clinicians agree that some memories may be inaccurate, that some memories of trauma may be lost from conscious awareness, and that it is possible to create inaccurate memories of past events. Also, as will become clear in later sections, memory researchers have moved beyond the study of every-day memory and have begun to creatively study the reconstructive nature of memory following stressful events.

Memories May Be Inaccurate

Memories are not always accurate and they are not immutable; rather they change depending on the present context. That is not to say that memories are always entirely false; they may contain elements of truth. However, the very process of retrieving a memory may create some distortions. Unfortunately, the science of memory is not refined enough for us to identify which or how much of a particular memory is accurate. It is not the purpose of this chapter to review the scientific literature on reconstructive memory (see British Psychological Society, 1995; Loftus, 1993; Yapko, 1994). However, psychotherapists should know basic information about memory processes.

Partisans on both sides of the false memory debate appear, at times, to argue in absolutes. Some writers appear to claim that having a memory of abuse always means that the abuse occurred or that the events represent abuse (although they recognize that the details or sequence of events may become jumbled). For example, Bass and Davis (1994) wrote:

> It is inevitable that survivors will remember the details of their abuse with some degree of inaccuracy. Time sequences may be mixed up, multiple incidents may be telescoped into a single incident, whole portions of incidents may be missing, and the events before and after may be blurred. *But the core of the memory, its emotional felt truth, has its own authenticity.* (p. 516, italics added)

Others imply that all memories retrieved during hypnosis are false and implanted. The actual truth is probably much more complicated. Behavioral scientists do not know enough about memory to verify, in the absence of corroborating evidence, which memories are accurate and which are false or implanted.

Memories May Become Lost

Some people can lose and later retrieve memories of past abuse. There are documented examples of patients who recalled past events spontaneously or through therapy and then later the perpetrator confessed or other corroborating evidence was found (Martinez-Taboas, 1996). Anecdotal data from the study of posttraumatic stress disorder provide other documented examples of people whose memories have been lost and later recovered. The complete loss of memory of traumatic events is atypical as most survivors keep re-experiencing the trauma through intrusive thoughts, nightmares, or startle reactions. Nevertheless, on describing World War II combat veterans, Grinker and Spiegel (1945) noted that some soldiers had

> total amnesia, including both events on the battlefield and the patient's previous life, or memory for part of the battle experience may be retained, with a gap involving the actual precipitating traumatic factors and the events that followed. The majority of patients make persistent attempts to recover their lost experiences, and in many instances their efforts may be successful without any aid from the therapist. (p. 10)

One particularly noteworthy study by Vardi (as cited in Brown, 1994) compared memory recall for adult women who reported childhood incest, adult women who reported rape as adults, and a control group of adult women. The incest survivors had significantly poorer recall for events occurring at the period of life associated with the incest, even for details irrelevant to the incest such as names of teachers or schools attended. Although the study did not address the issue of forgetting the abusive event, it does provide support for the theory that traumas may interfere with the typical process of memory.

Of course, the inability to retrieve memories associated with rape or incest may reflect the fact that because of the severe emotional distress connected with these events when they occurred, simultaneously occurring events were encoded inadequately. In this case, rather than entire memories of the event being repressed, only partial memories of events actually exist in memory. As a result, retrieval would be fragmented at best. This underscores the difference between lost memories that can be recovered and information that was never accurately stored in memory in the first place and thus by definition can never be recovered. Several research teams (Briere & Conte, 1993; Elliott & Briere, 1995; Feldman-Summers & Pope, 1994; Gold, Hughes, & Hohnecker, 1994; Herman & Schatzow, 1987; Loftus, Polonsky, & Fullilove, 1994; Sheiman, 1993; Williams, 1994) have found that many women reported having periods of time in which they were unable to recall past childhood abuse.

The frequency with which memories are lost is not known. At the present time, the frequencies with which memories are lost and later recovered is not known. The studies enumerated in the paragraph above in which women reported having lost and recovered memories of abuse have methodological limitations that suggest that the percentage of women who recalled lost memories is less than originally reported. For example, in some studies the women were asked ambiguous questions, such as "Was there ever a time when you could not remember some or all of the abuse?" A positive response may have indicated either that the patient avoided thinking about the abuse, had no memory of the abuse at all, or had failed to recall a minor detail concerning the abuse although she always recalled the general nature of the abuse. Some studies focused on patients who were in treatment to overcome the effects of traumas or presumed traumas, thus creating a nonrepresentative sample. Other studies included patients who had already been in psychotherapy and may have been exposed to memory recovery techniques that could have created false memories of abuse. Finally, there are limits to the confidence that may be placed in the conclusions drawn from surveys of psychotherapists about patients who report recovered memories when corroborating information is not available.

These criticisms are not meant to retract our previous statement that memories can be lost and later recalled. We believe that the anecdotal and verifiable clinical data strongly support the conclusion that some patients do lose and later regain memories of childhood abuse. Indeed the data in support of lost and recalled memories include a survey of psychotherapists that found that almost 1% of their patients regained lost memories of abuse (Pope & Tabachnick, 1995). Polusny and Follette (1996) found that 15% of psychologists had seen at least 1 case of lost and regained memory of childhood sexual abuse in the last year and another 4% had seen 5 or more cases.

The mechanisms by which memories are lost are unclear. The situations or mechanisms that cause important memories to be lost are not well understood. Some writers postulate that lost memories are due to repression. We will not review all the problems associated with the theoretical mechanism of repression; however, repression means different things to different writers. Even Freud used the term in different ways. Similar difficulties have been found with the terms *dissociation* and *amnesia*. Often writers appear to use those terms to refer to any type of forgetting.

Furthermore, repression, dissociation, and amnesia (however defined) are not the only mechanisms by which memories may be lost. Freyd (1994) has hypothesized *betrayal trauma* as a theoretical mechanism that attempts to explain lost memories as an adaptive response to childhood trauma. Van der Kolk (1995) has hypothesized that trauma may result in physiological or neuronal changes that impair the ability to store or retrieve information. It is also possible that memories are lost because of the ordinary process of memory decay or interference or because a patient consciously avoids thinking about the memory (Schacter, 1995). Future research may provide a better, more comprehensive and useful theory to explain the phenomena of lost memories of traumas.

False Memories May Be Created

A separate question concerns whether patients may develop false memories of past abuse. We believe that patients can, under certain circumstances, come to believe that they were abused when, in fact, they were not. The evidence in support of this assumption comes from the anecdotal and scientific literature on memory processes and the social psychological theories of social influence.

Anecdotal evidence. The most direct evidence of implanted memory comes from patient and therapist accounts of actual therapy session behaviors. Former patients, undercover agents posing as patients, and therapists' accounts of their own behavior all provide evidence that therapists may take symptom clusters, popular readings, symptom checklists, or sexualized dream interpretations to prove to a patient that she has lost her memories of being abused (Loftus, 1993). Furthermore, some of the allegations of abuse involve details that are so bizarre and unrealistic (intrauterine memories of abuse, UFO alien abduction abuse, etc.) that they stretch credibility. The bizarre nature of these allegations following a course of psychotherapy suggests that the psychotherapists implanted or at least encouraged a magnification of the false memories. Overall, the anecdotal evidence is extensive, but the case study methodology cannot prove cause and effect.

Memory research in support of the theory of iatrogenic memories. This quick review of the literature is only intended to briefly summarize several representative studies. Readers are referred elsewhere for more comprehensive reviews (British Psychological Society, 1995; Lindsay & Read, 1995; Loftus, 1993). Experimental studies on memory can be interpreted to support the theory of iatrogenic memory. These studies can more reliably demonstrate cause and effect relationships, although the extent to which simulated laboratory events apply to the real life memories of adults seeking psychotherapy is unclear. Nevertheless, the findings of false memory in laboratory studies through hypnotic suggestions, source misattribution, the recall of false events, or the recall of stressful events suggest that false memories can be created.

Hypnotic suggestions. Laurence and Perry (1983) tried to convince 27 hypnotized study participants that the participants had heard loud noises in the night that they had not initially reported. Of the 27 hypnotized participants, 13 became convinced that they had heard those noises, and 6 were unequivocal in their certainty. Even when debriefed and told that the memory of the noises was created through hypnosis, some study participants remained adamant that they had heard the noises. In another study, Spanos, Menary, Gabora, DuBreuil, and Dewhirst (1991) found that participants in a hypnotically induced past-life regression experiment were more likely to report child abuse in those past lives if they were given information about the frequency of childhood abuse in the past.

Source attribution. *Source attribution* refers to the ability of persons to accurately attribute the sources of the information they have acquired. Johnson and her colleagues (see review by Johnson, Hashtroudi, & Lindsay, 1993) found that people could become confused about the sources of certain information they acquired. For example, she found that research participants who were required to both imagine and to actually see various words were often unable to distinguish the sources of their exposure to the word.

Recall of false events. Hyman, Husband, and Billings (1995) asked parents of college students to report personal events that happened to their child before he or she reached the age of 10 (such as getting lost, going to a hospital, losing a pet, going on a family vacation, having an eventful birthday, or interacting with a prominent person). The researchers then asked these students to remember some events that never took place (having a visit from a clown during a birthday party, and going to the hospital with a high fever and possible ear infection). Although the students could not remember the false event during the first interview, 4 of the 20 participants "remembered" the false event in a subsequent interview.

Exposure to stressful events. Witnesses of stressful events sometimes develop stark inaccuracies in their memories of those events. For example, Neisser and Harsch (1993) asked college students to recall their memories of the disastrous Challenger space shuttle explosion. Many of the students reported that they learned about the disaster from friends and only about one fifth reported that they saw it live on television. However, when researchers interviewed the same students 2^1/$_2$ years later, 45% reported that they learned about the disaster from seeing it on television. Abhold (as cited in Loftus, 1993) studied spectators who watched a player experience cardiac arrest during a high school football game. The audience watched as paramedics apparently failed to resuscitate the player (he was later revived at the hospital). When interviewed 6 years later, many spectators committed serious errors in recalling the event. In response to a false suggestion, for example, one quarter of the spectators reported that they had seen blood on the jersey of the player. Finally, Pynoos and Nader (1989) studied the reaction of children to a sniper attack at their school. Even some of the children who were not at the school at the time of the attack reported detailed memories of the event. It appears that the memories were created by exposure to other children who had survived the attack.

All of the studies described in this section, dealing with hypnosis, source attribution, creation of false memories in college students, and distortions of stressful events, show that human memory is malleable and that average participants can be induced to believe events that did not occur. The major limitation of these studies is that they used research participants, and not people in actual psychotherapy. Nevertheless, the greater dependency of psychotherapy patients, coupled with their emotional distress, would seem to make them more vulnerable to having false memories implanted.

Social psychological support of the theory of iatrogenic memories. In addition to what is known about the processes of memory, social psychological influences can also help create iatrogenic memories. Table 2 lists several factors inherent in memory work procedures that increase the likelihood that false beliefs could be adopted (Lindsay & Read, 1995). Because patients may perceive their psychotherapists as benevolent and well-meaning, the therapists are in a position of trust to influence their patients. They may provide a motivation for the patient to recall the abuse ("it is necessary for you to recover"), and the patients are often anxious, lonely, depressed, or otherwise vulnerable to influence. Consequently, psychotherapists may be able to get them to agree

Table 2

Social Psychological Influences in Support of the Theory of Iatrogenic Memories

Influence	Application to Iatrogenic Psychotherapy
Source	Trusted authority (psychotherapist)
Motivation	It is necessary to recall the abuse to be healed
Acceptance of Plausibility	Explanation that presenting problems are symptoms of childhood abuse
	Explanation that denial or amnesia are symptoms of childhood abuse
Repeated Exposure	Through comments by psychotherapist, homework, suggestive bibliotherapy, and other influences
Group Support	Suggestive group therapy
Isolation	Recommendations to "detach" themselves from family members and other "toxic" persons who do not support their beliefs in abuse

to the plausibility of the hidden abuse premise ("other patients with your symptoms were able to identify hidden memories," or "you have the symptom profile of a person who was abused"). The patients may attend group meetings where they are supported or encouraged to adopt certain beliefs. Finally, they may be encouraged to detach themselves from family members or other "toxic" persons who do not support their beliefs. Many cases of alleged false memory have involved multiple sources of influence such as therapist suggestions (through leading questions, direct suggestions, suggestive interpretations of dreams, or interpretations of symptom clusters or checklists), hypnosis, suggestive bibliotherapy, survivor group meetings, marathon weekends, or "educational" seminars.

Other data in support of the theory of iatrogenic memories. Support for the premise that psychotherapists can create false memories of abuse in some patients comes from several other sources as well. Many psychotherapists believe that patients have false memories of abuse. A survey of psychologists by Pope and Tabachnick (1995) found that in about 12% of patients who recovered lost memories of abuse, either the psychotherapists or the patients concluded that the recovered memories were inaccurate.

Data from the False Memory Syndrome Foundation show that in 40% of the families who responded to a survey in their newsletter, the alleged perpetrators of sexual abuse were the mothers (Family Survey Update, 1994), although data from child protective authorities suggest that the frequency of sexual abuse by mothers is far less frequent than sexual abuse by fathers. In addition, Abrams and Abrams (as cited in Lindsay & Read, 1995) found that 78% of the 300 persons accused of childhood sexual abuse that did not involve recovered memories failed their lie detector tests. On the other hand, only 4% of the persons accused of childhood sexual abuse that did involve recovered memories failed their lie detector tests. Of course, these data must be seen as only suggestive and not conclusive, because lie detector tests are not accepted as completely reliable. Furthermore, it is possible that some of the alleged perpetrators may themselves have false memories of the past (Rubin, 1996).

Based on the cumulative evidence from anecdotes, studies of typical memory processes, our knowledge of social psychological influences on behavior, and other evidence, many experts believe that false memories of childhood events can be implanted. As the APA Working Group on the Investigation of Memories of Childhood Abuse concluded, "it is possible to construct convincing pseudomemories for events that never occurred" (Alpert et al., 1996, p. 1). There is, however, a legitimate controversy over the frequency with which false memories occur. As noted by Alpert, Brown, and Courtois (1996), memory research based on analogue studies often fails to include or replicate the important conditions present in therapy. Furthermore, the reliability of reports by retractors may need to be studied in more detail. Perhaps the retractors have unique features regarding suggestibility or memory function that led to their initial report and retraction.

Given the general agreement that implantation of false memories can occur, the accusation that a psychotherapist implanted a false memory of childhood abuse should not be dismissed automatically. Psychotherapists may find themselves charged with malpractice or an ethics violation if therapy leads the patient to conclude, without corroborating evidence, that she or he was abused and the therapist used highly suggestive diagnostic or treatment procedures that are described in later chapters. As suggested previously, it is therefore important that psychotherapists use techniques that are supported by the scientific and professional literature.

4

Risk Management: Diagnose Carefully

Both the principles of malpractice, described earlier, and the *Ethical Principles of Psychologists and Code of Conduct* of the American Psychological Association (APA, 1992) provide guidance for psychologists on matters of evaluation and assessment of patients who present with questions about childhood abuse. For example, Standard 1.06 of the ethics code states, "Psychologists rely on scientifically and professionally derived knowledge when making scientific or professional judgments or when engaging in scholarly or professional endeavors" (APA, 1992). Standard 2.01(b) states, "Psychologists' assessments, recommendations, reports, and psychological diagnostic or evaluative statements are based on information and techniques (including personal interviews of the individual when appropriate) sufficient to provide appropriate substantiation for their findings" (APA, 1992). Standard 2.02 reads in part:

> (a) Psychologists who develop, administer, score, interpret, or use psychological assessment techniques, interviews, tests, or instruments do so in a manner and for purposes that are appropriate in light of the research on or evidence of the usefulness and proper application of the techniques.
>
> (b) Psychologists refrain from misuse of assessment techniques, interventions, results, and interpretations and

take reasonable steps to prevent others from misusing the information these techniques provide.... (APA, 1992)

Finally, Standard 2.05 cautions:

When interpreting assessment results, including auto-mated interpretations, psychologists take into account the various test factors and characteristics of the person being assessed that might affect the psychologist's judg-ment or reduce the accuracy of their interpretations. They indicate any significant reservations they have about the accuracy or limitations of their interpretations. (APA, 1992)

Failure to follow these standards increases the risk that psy-chologists will be found in violation of the ethics code.

As noted previously, in a malpractice suit psychotherapists would be evaluated on the extent to which their diagnosis or treatment deviated from established professional standards. Many cases of malpractice have occurred when the psycho-therapists working within hospitals should have recognized suicidal or homicidal tendencies on the part of their patients and a suicide or assault occurred (see review by VandeCreek & Knapp, 1993). Judges and juries will not necessarily find a psychotherapist liable if a tragedy occurs; however, psycho-therapists may be found liable for failure to use profession-ally acceptable techniques in assessing the degree of danger. Similarly, judges and juries could find psychotherapists liable if they failed to use accepted professional techniques in as-certaining the actual problem of the patient and if the patient suffered harm as a consequence.

In this chapter we review some mistakes that psychother-apists can make when diagnosing patients that could lead to an overidentification of child abuse. We also identify two ad-ditional special subjects of concern in the area of diagnosis that are related to allegations of false memories. These in-clude the problem of managing patients who enter psycho-therapy with an expectation that psychotherapy will help them regain historically accurate memories and problems when diagnosing dissociative identity disorder. Finally, we comment on thinking or problem-solving styles that could systematically cause psychotherapists to misdiagnose their patients.

Standards for Identifying Past Abuse

Regardless of the stance that psychotherapists take regarding the recovery of memories, most agree that it is appropriate to ask patients about past abuse. It is just as appropriate to ask patients about past abuse as it is to ask them about marital status, domestic abuse, physical health, background of substance abuse, relationships with significant others, and other life circumstances. Evidence suggests that a background of past childhood abuse may be relevant to the type or severity of the presenting problem of the patient. For example, Romans, Martin, Anderson, Herbison, and Mullen (1995) found that 22 out of 23 women in a community sample who attempted suicide had backgrounds of childhood sexual abuse. The authors appropriately concluded that "good clinical practice should always consider the possibility of childhood sexual abuse when an adult woman is being assessed for self-destructive behavior or suicidal ideation" (p. 1341).

The asking or probing, as recommended by Romans et al. (1995) differs substantially from insisting there has been abuse or from using leading questions that suggest abuse. As described by Loftus and Ketcham (1994), some of the descriptions by recanters note that their psychotherapists asked them in the first session if they were abused as children. It is not always clear from these descriptions whether the psychotherapists were conducting a good initial interview by asking the patient a wide range of questions about their past history or whether the psychotherapists were suggesting that the patients were abused. Psychologists may be able to minimize confusion by identifying routine history gathering questions as such. In addition, Pope and Brown (1996) suggest that psychologists may phrase questions about sexual abuse in general terminology such as asking patients if they have ever had "any experiences in childhood that they found sexually inappropriate, uncomfortable, or frightening" (p. 158). This general phrasing allows patients to respond to a wide range of sexual experiences or feelings and reduces the likelihood that the patient would misunderstand what is meant by sexual abuse. This approach to interviewing also reduces the risk that the patient will later charge that the psychotherapist insisted or coerced the patient into claiming abuse.

Although childhood abuse may be related to the current psychopathology it should not be assumed that the distress of all adults is due to hidden childhood abuse. Unfortunately, some psychotherapists consider the identification of abuse as a "silver bullet" that is sufficient to cure the patient, if only the memory of abuse can be recovered. These psychotherapists use overly broad symptom checklists or definitions of childhood abuse and consider the failure to remember the abuse as denial. The emphasis on childhood abuse may lead to a misdiagnosis of the patient's actual condition and to substandard treatment. In addition, this may provide the basis for an ethics complaint (such as Standard 2.02 b cited earlier) and lead to charges of negligence.

Overidentification of Past Abuse

Some popular books tell readers to assume on the basis of symptoms alone that abuse did occur and then to work backwards to find the abuse. Maltz (1992) wrote, "If you sense you were sexually abused and have no memories of it, it's likely that you were" (p. 46). This quotation echoes the famous quote from *The Courage to Heal*, "If you think you were abused and your life shows the symptoms, then you were [abused]" (Bass & Davis, 1988, p. 22). In a later edition of the book, the authors modified their degree of certainty: "If you genuinely think you were abused and your life shows the symptoms, there's a strong likelihood that you were [abused]" (Bass & Davis, 1994, p. 26). Even the therapeutic attitude represented by that modification may lead to an overidentification of forgotten abuse. Although the Maltz and Bass and Davis books were written for a popular audience, these books are often used by psychotherapists as adjuncts to therapy. In such cases, psychotherapists may be tacitly supporting the assumption that sexual abuse can be identified on the basis of an unsubstantiated hunch or vague feeling.

The belief of some psychotherapists that child abuse causes most emotional problems is so strong that Yapko (1994) reported on one psychologist who claimed that she could identify an abused person just by talking with him or her casually for 10 minutes. Loftus and Ketcham (1994) reported that in some cases patients with suggestive symptom profiles have been informed by their clinicians, after a single consultation, that they were undoubtedly victims of abuse. Psychologists are encouraged to take seriously Standard 2.04(b) of the ethics code, which states that "psychologists recognize limits to the certainty with which diagnoses, judgments, or predictions can be made about individuals" (APA, 1992).

Overly Broad Definitions of Abuse

Other psychotherapists take an extremely broad definition of sexual abuse. Some writers such as Pendergast (1995) have used the term "emotional incest" to refer to clearly inappropriate acts, such as forcing teenage girls to change clothes in front of them, or other intrusive behavior that falls just short of physical incest. However, other psychotherapists use such broad definitions of emotional incest that it loses its usefulness as a concept. These definitions include accidentally walking in on another person in the bathroom, normal bathing of a child, or other actions that could be very understandable and innocuous in any family but that could be interpreted as pernicious if taken out of context. Although each of these examples could represent sexually inappropriate and offensive behavior, it is premature to conclude that emotional abuse occurred only on the basis of the events enumerated above. The boundary between appropriate and inappropriate behavior depends much on the perceived intent of the offender and the context in which the behavior occurs, such as whether it is part of a pattern or an isolated example.

Some psychotherapists may label symptoms as indications of past sexual abuse even when they are, at best, remotely related to possible abuse. For example, some psychotherapists have interpreted incidental characteristics, such as a fear of dentists, as an indicator of a body memory of having performed oral sex. As Fredrickson (1992) put it, "Extraordinary fear of dental visits is quite often a signal of oral sexual abuse, since it is reminiscent of being forced to open your mouth while something painful is done to it" (p. 43). Pendergast (1995) wrote about a psychotherapist who claimed that "sometimes a texture puts them off. Some people can't take anything that resembles semen—whipped cream, ice cream—and they don't know why. The conscious mind has just pushed the memories off to the side" (p. 212).

McNamara (1994) described a case of a clinician who allegedly reported that her patient "had seen a statue of a mother and infant in a courtyard at Massachusetts General Hospital. The mother's nakedness upset him.... [The psychiatrist] interpreted his response as a reaction to his mother's alleged sexual abuse" (p. 80). Of course, trauma survivors may develop aversion to certain stimuli that remind them of the trauma (Salter, 1995). However, it is not appropriate to work backwards and assume that any aversion is evidence of childhood abuse trauma. Bass and Davis (1988) stated that "many women don't have memories, and some never get memories. That doesn't mean they weren't abused" (p. 81). Davis later stated, "You can heal from the effects of abuse even if you never remember" (1990, p. 206). These statements, along with others, may encourage persons to perceive themselves as abused even in the absence of any evidence or memory.

Improper Use of Checklists

Another criterion used by Bass and Davis (1994), Fredrickson (1992), and others for determining if sexual abuse could have occurred is whether a reader responded positively to series of items on symptom checklists. To our knowledge, these checklists have not been subjected to psychometric evaluations for reliability and validity in identifying childhood abuse. For example, Bass and Davis (1994) wrote:

> Phobias, flashbacks, intrusive imagery, chronic patterns of denial and dissociation, flooding of feelings, spontaneous regression, startle reflexes, numbness in the body, and terror of sex may all point to a history of trauma in childhood. (p. 511)

Fredrickson (1992) presents a list of 63 symptoms, including such items as "I began masturbating at a very early age," "I showed no interest in sex until I was in my twenties," "I have difficulty falling or staying asleep," and "I neglect my teeth" (pp. 48–51). Readers are instructed,

> Check each item that applies to you, even if in a different way than the question indicates. There is no specific number of checkmarks needed to "prove" you have repressed memories. This list is only to help you start thinking about warning signals you may have missed or to validate signals that you feel might be clues to your abuse. (p. 47)

On their face the checklists appear to be undifferentiated measures of depression, anxiety, or stress and should not be used as sole indicators of child abuse. "If everything is a sign of past childhood sexual abuse, then nothing is" (Loftus, 1994, p. 444). Psychologists who rely for their diagnoses on checklists that have not been subjected to scientific scrutiny may be vulnerable to charges of violations of Standard 2.02(a), which states in part, "Psychologists who develop, administer, score, interpret, or use psychological assessment techniques, interviews, tests, or instruments do so in a manner and for purposes that are appropriate in light of the research on or evidence of the usefulness and proper application of the techniques" (APA, 1992).

Unfounded Belief in Symptoms Indicating Abuse

Polusny and Follette's survey (1996) found that some psychotherapists believe that there is a cluster of symptoms that can reliably identify a background of childhood abuse. "Of the 20% of respondents who do hold this belief, a wide range of adult symptoms were listed as clinical indicators" (p. 45). Unfortunately, no consensus exists among mental health professionals as to what that cluster of symptoms might be. No one symptom or symptom picture is pathognomic of abuse, because the abuse can range from mild to severe and because the context, age, and developmental stages of each child vary considerably (Pope & Brown, 1996).

Poole et al. (1995) found that many psychologists identified a cluster of symptoms that could allegedly indicate childhood sexual abuse in female patients. The most common symptoms listed were sexual dysfunction, poor relationships, low self-esteem, depression, amnesia for childhood memories, sleep disturbance, eating disorder, and dissociative symptoms. "... Most clinicians indicated that they had at least sometimes formed the opinion that a client who denied a history of CSA [childhood sexual abuse] had indeed been abused. A substantial minority of the clinicians indicated that they made this assessment quite frequently and that they sometimes did so very quickly" (p. 430). However, the most commonly identified symptom was listed by only 14% of the respondents, and their sample produced 85 different symptoms allegedly suggesting childhood sexual abuse. Similarly, Polusny and Follette (1996) found little agreement among psychologists concerning symptoms that indicate childhood abuse. Clearly, a standard of care does not yet exist in this area of assessment and diagnosis, and psychologists should exercise caution about drawing firm conclusions based on weak data.

Overemphasis on Denial

The failure to remember abuse or to express any doubt of being abused is, according to some psychotherapists, a symptom of denial and further evidence of the intensity of the past abuse and repression. Numerous patients have struggled against the accusation that they were in denial. One of the authors [S.K.] had a conversation with a patient who was in great distress. The patient said,

> My therapist has helped me a great deal over the last 10 years. I value his support and insight, but he insists that I was a victim of SRA [satanic ritual abuse]. I don't have any memories of this. He wants to put me into a therapy group where they will confront my denial. But I don't think I was abused. Whenever I spoke with him about this, he pounded his fists on his desk and said, "Denial! Denial! Denial!"

Another former patient wrote, "If I did not behave in a way conducive to what he or the staff believed, I was 'in denial,' and 'regressing,' and I would be denied any privileges, like using the telephone or even sleeping in a bed" (Pendergast, 1995, p. 349). Yet another former patient is quoted by the *FMS Foundation Newsletter* as writing, "From the minute I walked in her door, her agenda was sexual abuse by my father.... That's all we talked about. I remember saying to her, 'I was never sexually abused by my father.' But she just kept at it" (Scanlon, 1994, p. 7). And still another former patient is quoted by the *FMS Foundation Newsletter* as stating

> My therapist's conjecture of incest became a recurring mental boxing match because of its very nature: I believed it was preposterous, yet one of the hallmarks of such abuse is supposed to be its denial. Was I sure it never happened? (Overstreet, 1993, p. 6)

In another variation, some therapists may lead patients who had always recalled past abuse to find additional instances of abuse. Schwarz (1996) refers to this phenomena as *magnification* and related an instance in which a patient who had always known she had been sexually abused as a child became upset when she read an article about satanic ritualistic abuse. When she told this to her therapist, he suggested that it meant that she had been a victim of ritualistic sexual abuse.

Kluft wrote that "the documenting of one abuse allegation should not be held as proving that other allegations are founded, and the disconfirming of one abuse allegation should not be held as demonstrating that other allegations are erroneous" (1996, p. 106). Fortunately, many patients question the quick conclusions of their psychotherapists. However, many patients enter psychotherapy in a highly suggestive and vulnerable state and may accept their psychotherapist's explanation of their problems without question.

An Alternative View of Diagnosis

A determination of childhood abuse should never be made on the basis of a cluster of symptoms alone. Depression, suspiciousness, anxiety, and other symptoms can be caused by several factors, of which childhood sexual abuse is only one. The plausibility of childhood abuse does not mean that it is likely or inevitable. Being overly quick to identify childhood sexual abuse does a disservice to the patient, may reflect a bias on the part of the psychotherapist, and may place the psychotherapist at risk of violating Standard 2.01(b) of the ethics code (APA, 1992).

Furthermore, abuse is not a diagnosis; it is a past event which may, or may not, be related to the patient's current problems. Guthiel (1993) warned that "a facile formulation of 'child sexual abuse' may replace a careful clinical assessment of a complex history" (p. 529). Consideration should be given to alternative explanations of the problems of the patient (Bloom, 1994).

Finally, a good treatment plan depends on many factors, and identifying possible past abuse is seldom, in and of itself, an adequate treatment plan. Nevertheless, Bass and Davis stated that "reliving a memory is part of your healing" (1994, p. 88), and Fredrickson (1992) stated that "the bulk of your repressed memories need to be identified, retrieved, and debriefed for healing to occur" (p. 223). However, to our knowledge, these statements have no empirical support. Even if abuse did occur, there is no proof that the identification, reliving, or disclosure of the abuse is necessary for a successful treatment. Only 13% of psychologists believe it is very important to remember sexual abuse to alleviate the symptoms of adult distress (Polusny & Follette, 1996). According to Terr (1994), "The success of treatment does not depend on the retrieval of memories the way the success of a fishing expedition depends on the catching of fish. One does not have to uncover a buried memory in order to feel better and perform better" (pp. 160–161). According to the APA Working Group on Investigation of Memories of Childhood Abuse (Alpert et al., 1996), "The goal of therapy is not archeology; recollection of trauma is only helpful insofar as it is integrated into a therapy emphasizing improvement of functioning" (p. 5).

Finally, Harvey and Herman (1994) drew a similar conclusion about the goal of uncovering memories. They stated,

> Contrary to the portrait of clinical work with trauma survivors being promulgated by the popular press and the false memory literature, the aim of clinical exploration of the traumatic past is neither to uncover more and more horror, nor to assign blame and responsibility for adult life to others, but rather to help the adult survivor name and assign meaning and comprehensibility to the past, to facilitate the integration of traumatic remembrance into an ongoing personal narrative, and to help the patient grieve the past and be free of it. (p. 304)

Child Abuse and Later Psychopathology

A background of childhood abuse is one of many factors that could be related to the diagnosis or presenting problem of the patient. Although honest scientific differences exist concerning the relative contribution of childhood abuse to later psychopathology, most authorities agree that self-reported childhood sexual abuse is correlated with psychopathology among adults, especially for depression, anxiety, and eating and personality disorders (Alpert, Brown, & Courtois, 1996; American Psychiatric Association, 1993; Becker et al., 1995; British Psychological Society, 1995). Finkelhor and Dzubia-Leatherman (1994) claimed that abused children are four times more likely to develop psychopathology than children who are not abused.

However, the correlation of childhood abuse with later psychopathology does not mean that clinicians can work backwards and assume that the presence of a mental disorder means that the person was abused as a child. For example, Silk, Lee, Hill, and Lohr (1995) found that 76% of the patients diagnosed with borderline personality disorder reported sexual abuse as a child. Their definition of sexual abuse was broad. Based on their data, a clinician who assumed that sexual abuse occurred simply because her patient had borderline personality disorder would be incorrect almost one fourth of the time.

In addition, the correlation of childhood abuse with later psychopathology does not prove that the child abuse necessarily caused the psychopathology. The abuse may reflect a lack of adequate boundaries between parents and children in a wide range of situations, not just in sexual behavior. As children, they also may have lacked adequate parental investment to help them adjust to their normal developmental tasks. Furthermore, because the self-reports of sexual abuse are often made retrospectively, there is a methodological limitation on the ability to ascertain a cause and effect relationship. Prospective studies or studies that involve objective verification of the abuse are more useful in determining a cause and effect relationship. During periods of depression or stress, patients may selectively recall or magnify examples of poor parenting and overidentify themselves as abused children in an effort to explain their present problems.

In addition, child abuse does not necessarily cause lasting harm for all individuals (Beutler, Williams, & Zetzer, 1994). Some survivors have even claimed that the experience made them stronger (McMillen, Zuravin, & Rideout, 1995), although some of the "benefits" may have come from the sequelae of the abuse (such as expressions of support from family members), as opposed to the abuse itself.

Most important, the correlation between childhood abuse and later psychopathology does not mean that all, or even most adult difficulties originate from childhood traumas. Mental illness can still occur in the absence of childhood trauma. Other stresses, personal vulnerabilities, cognitive styles, and biological predisposition also play a role in the development of psychopathology. Furthermore, the presence of sexual abuse in the history of a patient does not necessarily mean that a particular diagnostic pattern or set of symptoms will be present.

Unfortunately, reports have emerged of patients who received inappropriate treatment based on a theory that their problems were due to repressed memories. McElroy and Keck (1995) reported on a patient with obsessive–compulsive disorder (OCD) who was encouraged to reflect on her past (and repressed) history of abuse. Not surprisingly, she failed to improve with what the authors called "recovered memory therapy." Similarly, Lipinski and Pope (1994) described patients with obsessional disorders who were diagnosed as having flashbacks of repressed childhood trauma because of intrusive memories of stabbings, corpses, and mutilations. However, their obsessive symptoms disappeared and their compulsive behavior stopped when they were placed on medications. Lief and Fetkewicz (1995) similarly described a patient with flashbacks of abuse who was subsequently diagnosed with OCD. OCD represents a cluster of disorders which probably have a biological basis or genetic predisposition for which behavior therapy or medication is the most appropriate treatment (Knapp & VandeCreek, 1994). Attributing obsessive–compulsive behaviors to repressed memories of abuse falls below the minimal standards of competence expected of psychotherapists and places them in jeopardy of being charged with negligence.

Bass and Davis (1994) quoted one "survivor" who, although she could not remember being abused, became convinced that she had been. She asked herself, "why would I be feeling all of this? Why would I be feeling all this anxiety if something didn't happen? If the specifics are not available to you, then go with what you've got" (p. 92). The comments of this woman appear to be an effort after meaning. However, a responsible psychotherapist should avoid promoting hidden sexual abuse as a likely cause of all emotional distress.

Patients Who Request Help in Recovering Memories

As the media popularizes the possibility of recovering memories through hypnosis and other techniques, prospective patients may ask psychotherapists to diagnose them as survivors of childhood abuse and help them retrieve memories of childhood events or to verify their vague recollections or feelings of abuse. Polusny and Follette (1996) found a substantial increase in one year in the number of psychologists who reported that more patients were reporting childhood sexual abuse and that more patients were presenting for therapy with the goal of remembering childhood sexual abuse.

Although the attribution of such power to retrieve memories is flattering, prudent psychotherapists acknowledge the limitations of their techniques. They will disavow any such infallible skill, noting that memory is a reconstructive process and that no truth serum, be it hypnosis or drugs, is without shortcomings. Such a stance also reduces the risk that the psychologist will be found in violation of the ethics code (APA, 1992) or that the criteria for a malpractice suit will be met.

Patients may become angry with a therapist who disavows the ability to provide a truth serum, or who expresses uncertainty about the literal truth of the childhood memories that patients may recall. In addition, psychotherapists may feel an urge to help patients in serious distress by reassuring them "of the absolute accuracy of what is being remembered or by using techniques that appear to move towards quicker and more absolute certainty" (Pope & Brown, 1996, p. 147). Nevertheless, patients are better off with a therapist who honestly holds judgment in abeyance. Clinical skill is required to balance the patient's need for emotional support with the need to remain open to alternative explanations in the presence of ambiguous or conflicting evidence. Humility and caution are needed here as with any patient. Psychotherapists should not be afraid to express uncertainty about the etiology of a particular problem. Symptomatology can be multidetermined, and it should not be presumed that similar symptoms in different patients have the same etiology.

Some patients may not be able to confirm their inklings or suspicion of past abuse. They may be better off living with uncertainty and ambiguity than rushing to ill-conceived conclusions about their past. Treatment may help these patients adjust to this unresolved area of their lives. "Both patients and therapists, in some cases for a limited period of time and in some cases on a permanent basis, must tolerate uncertainty about the historical reality of memory production" (Alpert, Brown, & Courtois, 1996, p. 76).

Special Problems in Diagnosing Dissociative Identity Disorder

Serious childhood trauma is one of the common antecedents of dissociative identity disorder (formerly multiple personality disorder). However, as noted above, psychotherapists may be liable for making faulty diagnoses of patients. According to a popular press account by Keenan (1995), court records indicated that one specialist in dissociative identity disorder reportedly had seven lawsuits filed against him for negligent treatment and diagnosis. Another psychiatrist had a multimillion dollar judgment against her for allegedly inducing a patient to believe that she had a dissociative identity disorder (*Hamanne v. Humenansky*, 1995).

Many mental health professionals disagree concerning the frequency or even the existence of dissociative identity disorder. Its reported frequency in different psychiatric settings varies from 2.4 to 35% depending on the study (Latz, Kramer, & Hughes, 1995). Some specialists believe that dissociative identity disorder does not exist at all, but rather is an artifact of misguided psychotherapy (McHugh, 1993). Clinicians may find themselves in legal jeopardy if they take an unusually broad interpretation of dissociative identity disorder, fail to identify other more prosaic diagnoses, or are perceived as encouraging patients to develop dissociative symptoms. Freeland, Manchanda, Chiu, Sharma, and Merskey (1993) documented four cases in which patients presented themselves as having multiple personality disorders, but did not improve until they were given another diagnosis and treated accordingly. The patients appeared to have acquired these diagnoses from the popular media or from contact with previous psychotherapists.

From a risk management perspective, psychotherapists should carefully document the symptoms and clinical indices that lead them to identify dissociative identity disorder. Care must be taken to avoid suggesting symptoms to a patient, and attention should be given to possible media contamination (through reading popular books or watching popular talk shows) by patients who present themselves as having a multiple personality disorder.

The Psychology of Clinical Judgment

Why would well-meaning and well-trained psychotherapists develop diagnostic methods and assumptions that may overidentify or magnify the importance of childhood abuse? The answer may be that, as much as psychotherapy should be based on the scientifically derived principles of behavioral science, by necessity psychotherapy requires considerable judgment, and psychotherapists may fall prey to the same fallacies of human judgment that befall all humans.

The insights developed by psychotherapists are valuable tools that help them perform at their optimal level. However, these useful insights may become harmful biases or prejudices if they are based on faulty reasoning. For example, it may be incorrect to identify a pattern based on a few or several examples. Poole et al. (1995) found that 48% of psychologists in one sample believed that sexual dysfunction could indicate a background of childhood sexual abuse. That insight could be useful because research shows that adult survivors of childhood sexual abuse have higher rates of sexual dysfunction than adults who were not abused. However, the knowledge of the relationship between sexual dysfunction and childhood abuse could become a harmful bias or prejudice if the psychotherapist failed to realize that most patients with sexual dysfunction were not sexually abused as children, and that many persons who were sexually abused as children do not have current sexual dysfunction. In other words, psychotherapists should not interpret the low correlation between sexual dysfunction and childhood sexual abuse to mean that patients with sexual dysfunction were abused as children.

Knowledgeable psychotherapists do not confuse correlation with causation. An erroneous assumption could be made by a psychotherapist who had a few or several patients in whom sexual dysfunction was found in concert with a background of child sexual abuse. These psychotherapists may fall victim to prejudice by assuming that sexual dysfunction always occurs because of a background of childhood sexual abuse. When psychotherapists develop a belief in the causation between abuse and psychopathology, they may develop a confirmatory bias, whereby they remember cases that support their hypotheses and discard or qualify cases that do not support it.

Another pitfall is that psychotherapists may give too much weight to a few dramatic or highly emotional case examples. They may consider highly vivid or dramatic examples to be representative of all patients when, in fact, they are not. The fact that a few or several patients recovered from a psychological disorder after recalling past events of childhood abuse does not mean that all patients will improve after recalling lost events.

Another potential problem in diagnosis includes the fundamental attribution error. As applied to clinical decision making, in the fundamental attribution error the psychologist may look for factors within the person that influence behavior and ignore present stressors. The clinician may interpret symptoms as being a sign of possible childhood abuse and ignore the impact of present circumstances on the behaviors, thoughts, and emotions of the patient.

Psychotherapists should also be careful about overinterpreting a finding of significant differences between groups. Two groups (adults who were abused or not abused as children, for example) may show significant difference in the presence of one particular symptom. However, this does not mean that symptom can be used to reliably identify one particular individual. A simple illustration can demonstrate the problems associated with overuse of occasional symptoms as predictors of repressed childhood abuse. Assume for the sake of illustration that 1% of all psychotherapy patients have lost memories of childhood abuse (this is the percentage of patients of psychologists who had lost and recovered memories of abuse as reported by Pope & Tabachnick, 1995). Also assume that the use of occasional symptoms as indicators of childhood abuse will lead to a 2% false positive rate (in this example a false positive refers to the identification of a lost memory of abuse in a person who was not abused). Given these assumptions, then out of a sample of 200,000 patients, 1%, or 2,000 patients, will recover lost memories of actual childhood abuse. However, 2% of the other 198,000 patients, or 3,960 patients, will be assumed to have lost memories of childhood abuse when, in fact, they were never abused.

We chose the 2% false positive rate arbitrarily, and it was not intended to reflect any responsible estimate of the frequency of false positive. However, we did select a low number to show how even a small false positive rate can affect a large number of patients.

Conclusions

The risk of premature or inaccurate identification of childhood abuse is enhanced by the increased number of patients who enter psychotherapy with a goal of trying to remember past childhood sexual abuse (Polusny & Follette, 1996). However, the identification of the appropriate diagnosis or presenting problem is one of the most, if not the most, important functions of an effective psychotherapist. Psychologists need to take special care in reaching their diagnoses and avoid the critical thinking errors that could result in inappropriate or inaccurate diagnoses. A diagnosis that is based on acceptable professional standards would greatly reduce the likelihood of a successful malpractice suit or ethics charge.

5

Risk Management: Conduct Good Psychotherapy

As noted in chapter 2, charges of negligence are likely to occur when patients experience negative outcomes and when they have ill feelings toward the psychotherapist. Good psychotherapy requires using effective techniques in the context of a respectful and collaborative relationship that enables patients to become autonomous and confident.

Judges and juries are more likely to find psychotherapists liable for choosing not widely accepted interventions when the harm has been obvious, such as when patients act on suicidal or homicidal tendencies, or disrupt family relationships. For example, McNamara (1994) reported on the case of a psychiatrist who was sued for malpractice when she helped a patient recover lost memories of sexual abuse and then the patient later killed himself. The unproven reparenting treatment procedure was allegedly inappropriate for the patient whom other experts claimed was suffering from a psychotic depression.

In addition, treatments need to be reconsidered if the patient is not improving. In *Osheroff v. Chestnut Hill Lodge* (1985), the patient sued because he was allegedly given intensive psychotherapy for his depression over many years and, despite his failure to improve, was never informed of alternative treatments such as medication. Anytime that a patient fails to improve despite the competent implementation of a treatment plan, strong consideration should be given to alternative diagnoses or treatment plans or alternative treatment providers.

In the event of a lawsuit based on a lost memory of abuse or an allegation of a falsely implanted memory of abuse, judges will look to experts in psychotherapy and memory research to guide them as to the proper professional and scientific standards. One of the sources of guidance courts will look to are the ethical codes of the respective psychotherapy professions. Each of these codes recognizes the need to keep appropriate boundaries between the psychotherapist and patient.

This chapter will review ethical and professional standards related to professional boundaries, the use (if any) of techniques designed to recover memories, adjuncts to treatment, informed consent, and relationships with the family members of patients.

Maintaining Proper Boundaries With Patients

According to the American Psychological Association ethics code (APA, 1992), psychologists are required to avoid multiple relationships with patients that may compromise their objectivity (boundary violations). As noted in previous chapters, some recanters have reported harmful boundary crossings by a therapist such as socializing with patients at a party or having a patient recruit registrants for the therapist's workshops. Patients who have been abused have already experienced boundary violations with their abusers, so psychotherapists should be especially vigilant about maintaining a professional relationship.

A Positive Professional Relationship

It is important to maintain a collaborative therapeutic relationship with patients. The psychotherapist should provide patients with as much control as possible and affirm their capacity to make good choices. The principle of patient control and patient–therapist collaboration means that a psychotherapist should not use highly suggestive statements or leading questions or pressure the patient to accept the therapist's hypothesis about the source of the problems. Overuse of interpretation reinforces the contraindicated notion of the wise psychotherapist and the ignorant, naive, or dependent patient. As with other charges of negligence, patients may be more willing (or even eager) to sue if the therapeutic relationship was weak. This is especially true if patients felt that their psychotherapists talked down to them, assumed a smug sense of superiority, or demeaned their ability to understand and address their own problems.

Always discounting the patient's failure to recall past events as denial may be an example of disrespect for the patient's experiences and perceptions. No scientific test can determine if a patient is repressing or denying an event. Psychotherapists have to judge when a patient is resistant and when or how to confront that patient. Sometimes resistance is healthy; sometimes patients deny events because they really never happened.

Appropriate Boundaries

No one contends that every contact with a patient outside of the office is necessarily an ethical violation. The *Ethical Principles of Psychologists and Code of Conduct* (APA, 1992) acknowledges that some contacts with patients may occur outside of the office through incidental or unavoidable circumstances. Furthermore, it could be appropriate for psychotherapists to conduct some therapeutic techniques, such as in vivo desensitization, outside of the office. However, the boundary crossings described previously by the recanters do not fall into any of these categories. In addition, they may have been perceived by patients as efforts on the part of the psychotherapists to gratify themselves or fulfill political and social agendas at the expense of the therapeutic relationship.

Most of the existing malpractice litigation on boundary violations concerns direct sexual contact between patients and psychotherapists. Strassburger, Jorgenson, and Sutherland (1992) have analyzed cases of sexual contact between patients and psychotherapists and noted that they frequently occurred after a series of boundary violations starting with subtle boundary crossings (e.g., exchanging gifts, excessive self-disclosure on the part of the therapist) and moving on to more obvious boundary violations (e.g., attending social gatherings together).

One of the earliest cases on psychiatrist–patient sex noted that sexual contact took place after the psychiatrist invited the patient to his house for parties and nude swimming, and they had gone on vacations together. The court ruled that "the damage would have been done to [the patient] even if the trips outside the state were carefully chaperoned, the swimming done with swimming suits on, and if there had been ballroom dancing instead of sexual relations" (*Zipkin v. Freeman*, 1968, p. 761).

Boundary violations include areas other than sexual contact. A patient wrote that her therapist

> used to hold me in his lap after those [anger] episodes—
> nothing sexual, but he felt like he needed to heal my
> inner child. He used to encourage me to make phone
> calls to him, because I would be shook up the next day.
> One time he threw a bucket of water at my head. Many
> times, he had to slap me really hard. I didn't think it was
> wrong for him to hit me. If he hit me, it meant he loved
> me. (Pendergast, 1995, p. 259)

In another case a psychiatrist allegedly had long and frequent discussions of her own emotional problems with the patient, had directed another member of the therapy group to give the patient a full body massage, and had ordered the patient "and her husband to move furniture and files, perform office and billing chores and assist in the 'treatment' of others" (*Hamanne v. Humenansky*, 1995, p. 10).

Moreover, boundary violations also include any use of the patient that gratifies the therapist's needs at the expense of those of the patient (Briere, 1992). Some boundary confusion is more subtle, such as encouraging patients to "detach" from their families, forbidding patients to contact their families, pressuring patients to confront their perpetrators publicly, or in other ways aligning too closely with the patient by, for example, championing the rights of the abused regardless of the needs of the patients. Pope and his colleagues refer to such actions as "intrusive advocacy" and claim that it could occur when a well-meaning therapist is "inattentive to issues of power and motivation, [and] becomes overly active in attempts to persuade a client to bring or to not bring a lawsuit or complaint" (Pope & Brown, 1996, p. 224).

Other therapists have reportedly discouraged or prohibited their patients from having romantic relationships during the course of psychotherapy. As reported by one psychotherapist,

> Sometimes, when the memories are too difficult to face, women still unconsciously try to derail the therapy process. . . . The next thing you know, something outside therapy makes them pay total attention to it. They go out and fall in love, right then. Sometimes I tell people, "Look this might delay things for a year." (Pendergast, 1995, pp. 216–217)

Psychotherapists who become strong advocates for the rights of victims risk losing their objectivity. Advocacy may be related to a tendency toward overidentification "when the therapist's empathic response to a client is unconsciously intensified by his or her own abuse-oriented affects and cognitions" (Briere, 1992, p. 159). Some psychotherapists may become overinvested in soothing the patient or punishing the offender. According to the code of ethics of the American Psychiatric Association (1986), "The psychiatrist should not use the unique position of power afforded him/her by the psychotherapeutic situation to influence the patient in any way not directly relevant to the treatment goal" (Section 2-2). Because public advocacy includes many unique features, it is discussed in greater detail in the section below on Showing Concern for Family Relationships.

Other examples of boundary confusion include inappropriate personal disclosures during therapy or excessively intrusive questions. Overly intrusive questions that smack of psychological voyeurism may cause a resurgence of the trauma and the patient may no longer consider the therapeutic setting as a safe environment. As will be documented below, boundary violations appear to be a factor in other problem areas of work with these patients as well, such as faulty diagnoses and selecting an improper treatment technique. Psychotherapists should be especially alert to maintaining boundaries with patients who have been abused because these patients have already been victims of boundary violations. Many such patients can be expected to reenact boundary problems in their relationships with their psychotherapists. The report of the American Psychiatric Association (1993) on memories of sexual abuse states that

> psychiatrists should vigilantly assess the impact of their conduct on the boundaries of the doctor/patient relationship. This is especially critical when treating patients who are seeking care for conditions that are associated with boundary violations in the past. (p. 5)

The recanters studied by Lief and Fetkewicz (1995) reported unusually close relationships between themselves and their psychotherapists. Of the 40 recanters, 36 (90%) reported telephoning their therapists between sessions, 15 (37.5%) telephoned them every day, and 24 (60%) wrote to them between sessions. Experienced clinicians know that, under unusual circumstances, it could be clinically indicated for psychotherapists to allow such dependency. However, as the Lief and Fetkewicz survey indicates, such dependency is fraught with potential problems and may lead patients to perceive that the psychotherapists are overly involved in their lives.

The failure to maintain appropriate boundaries not only can undermine therapeutic effectiveness, but it can also anger the patient enough to precipitate a lawsuit. Many survivors of abuse vary between idealization and vilification of others, including their therapists. Goldstein and Farmer (1993) describe one recanter who wrote about her idolization of her therapist and the blurring of boundaries:

> I believed in him so deeply. I began telling other people, "Trust him, believe in him, he will make you whole." I believed in him so completely, in 1986 I spent five months coordinating a retreat for women suffering from bulimia. In a five-month period, I talked with over 350 women suffering from this disorder. I wanted them all to know about Steve. Of course, Steve lectured. If Steve said it, I believed it. (p. 353)

Later she sued Steve and others whom she believed had implanted false memories of child abuse.

Patient Challenges to Boundaries

Because of the challenging behavior of some patients, maintaining boundaries may be one of the hardest tasks for psychotherapists. The psychotherapy relationship may be the patient's first nonexploitative intimate relationship. The "notion that psychotherapy is for the client, not the therapist, is often hard for the survivor to apprehend—especially given his or her experience with exploitative relationships in the past" (Briere, 1992, p. 89). Furthermore, the relationship may be characterized by extreme transference reactions on the part of the patient. The patient may project onto the psychotherapist the status of a rescuer, oppressor, or potential lover. Failure to meet these expectations can engender a crisis in the therapeutic relationship.

Some seriously disturbed patients become angry when the therapist sets clear boundaries. According to Mayer (1995), when he set reasonable boundaries with one of his patients, she accused him of violating her just as her father did when he raped her. His "offense" was that he had another appointment waiting and he had to bring the interview to a close. When therapists maintain appropriate boundaries, some of the more difficult patients or survivors may retaliate by stopping payment on checks, threatening lawsuits, or attacking the competency or compassion of the psychotherapist. Although it is not considered a treatment success when such patients leave therapy, they are better off with a therapist who maintains boundaries as a condition of psychotherapy than with one who is intimidated or cajoled into bending or breaking boundaries.

Choosing the Right Intervention

Another obviously important ingredient of effective psychotherapy is the choice of the proper intervention. Interventions should have their success measured by controlled outcome studies or in other ways be professionally derived. They should also be consistent with what is known about the scientific basis of memory acquisition, retention, and distortions (see review in chapter 3, this volume).

Unfortunately, outcome data do not exist to guide every diagnostic or psychotherapeutic decision. For example, although cognitive therapy has been shown through outcome studies to be highly effective in treating depression, the characteristics of the patient (age, sex, personal strengths, secondary or tertiary diagnoses, etc.) may limit the generalizability of those particular studies. Consequently, psychotherapists often will need to make clinical decisions based on their best professional judgment, without the benefit of outcome studies to guide their decisions. Nevertheless, as much as possible, data should drive treatment decisions. As detailed below, many of the techniques commonly used to retrieve past memories do not have scientific support for their ability to retrieve accurate memories or to effectively treat the disorders of the patients.

The first step in becoming an effective psychotherapist for adult survivors of childhood abuse is to become familiar with the scientific literature on reconstructive memory and forgotten past events or traumas. Psychotherapists whose diagnostic and treatment procedures are based on, or are consistent with, a sound understanding of their scientific basis need have little fear of creating or magnifying memories of childhood abuse.

Systematically Assessing Patient Care

In addition to using techniques based on outcome data, prudent psychotherapists systematically review the quality of their services to their own patients. Even if psychotherapists know and understand the treatment protocols well, actual quality control mechanisms or outcome data gathered on their own patients may help determine if they are implementing the intervention as intended. This will also help determine if their patient population has certain characteristics that prevent generalizing the findings of the outcome studies to their patients.

Some psychotherapists mistakenly believe that outcome programs have to be highly expensive, time-consuming, and complicated. However, collecting and recording data in a systematic manner can provide a body of useful information without being overly burdensome. Basic patient satisfaction surveys and standardized outcome measures are available at relatively low cost in terms of both money and time.

Quality can also be assessed systematically by an outside professional who may make a random case chart review. The professional who is doing the review should be one who has credentials, experiences, or expertise to provide a meaningful review of work with these patients. In addition, psychotherapists who are attracting a large portion of patients with lost and recovered memories of abuse may want to discuss their techniques with colleagues to determine if they are unwittingly steering their patients to recover lost memories (Schneider, 1994).

Outcome Studies With Adult Survivors of Childhood Abuse

Little outcome research has been done specifically with adult survivors of childhood abuse. Instead, most outcome research focuses on the treatment of specific diagnostic categories, such as depression, anxiety, personality disorders, or similar categories.

Psychotherapy outcome studies of adult survivors of childhood abuse have found significant improvement for the participants (see review by Becker et al., 1995). However, these studies have many methodological limitations such as lack of control groups, heterogeneous diagnostic categories represented in the patient population, and variability in outcome measurements. Furthermore, these studies have focused primarily on sexual abuse with women, and not on other types of abuse or abuse against men.

To date, outcome data are not available to provide clear treatment decisions for all adult survivors. Nevertheless, psychotherapists can feel very safe in choosing empirically supported treatments or professionally accepted treatments according to the diagnostic category of the particular patient. As with all treatments, modifications will have to be made to fit the needs of the individual patient.

Patient Challenges to Quality Care

Sometimes patients enter psychotherapy with preconceived notions of what constitutes good psychotherapy. As mentioned above, some patients may expect their psychotherapists to help them recover memories of past traumas. Other patients may expect their psychotherapists to encourage intense emotional experiences and feel surprised when their psychotherapists instead focus on social skills intervention, relationship enhancement with significant others, or cognitive restructuring. Still other patients may expect virtually unrestricted access to their psychotherapists. One self-help book offers the following advice to prospective patients:

> Look for a therapist who is flexible, especially initially. Sessions with trauma survivors often need to be from two to four hours long.... Initial therapy may bring up many issues simultaneously and so may require several visits a week. Experienced therapists understand and accommodate these needs. (Oksana, 1994, p. 279)

Because of these counter-therapeutic expectations on the part of some patients, psychotherapists may need to spend extra time explaining the purpose, procedures, and parameters of psychotherapy and addressing inappropriate expectations.

Outcomes With Memory Retrieval Techniques

When treating adult survivors of childhood abuse, psychotherapists must adhere to the ethical principles of their respective professions and follow acceptable professional standards in diagnosing and treating their patients. Caution in using unproven techniques is an aspirational goal under the code of ethics of the APA (1992):

> In those areas in which recognized professional standards do not yet exist, psychologists exercise careful judgment and take appropriate precautions to protect the welfare of those with whom they work. (General Principle A: Competence)

Also, Standard 1.04(c) of the code (APA, 1992) cautions psychologists about using unproven techniques.

As will be documented below, our review of the outcome literature suggests that memory-focused hypnosis or sodium amytal interviews, age regression, interpretation of memory fragments, body work, and other techniques have little or no empirical evidence to justify their effectiveness in retrieving accurate memories. Furthermore, we believe that they can lead to inaccurate memories in some cases and do not encourage their use. If psychotherapists do decide to use them in highly selective circumstances, we suggest they include specific procedural safeguards that reduce the likelihood of iatrogenic effects.

Hypnosis

Hypnosis has a long history of use within the American judicial system, mostly regarding hypnotically refreshed memories of witnesses of crimes. Generally speaking, courts have taken a skeptical attitude toward the admission of evidence generated or refreshed by hypnosis. Some judges will not accept hypnotically induced memories at all. Others will do so only if certain safeguards have been met. The most common safeguards are that the hypnotist was appropriately qualified, avoided adding new elements to the patient's story, made a permanent record of the hypnosis (either audio or video recording), demonstrated that suggestive procedures were not used, and provided other evidence that corroborated the hypnotically enhanced testimony (Scheflin & Shapiro, 1989).

As applied to childhood memories, hypnosis is regarded by many experts as incapable of producing accurate memories of the past. Hypnosis "as a memory-enhancement or memory-retrieval strategy seems questionable at best" (Pope & Brown, 1996, p. 59). Although hypnosis may produce an increase in memories, many of the memories are false; but patients will develop *concreting*, or a tendency to adamantly regard the created memories as accurate (Spanos, Burgess, & Burgess, 1994). Hypnosis may be especially problematic with highly suggestible patients or if it is used with suggestive commands or inductions (Lindsay & Read, 1995). Out of the 20 recanters surveyed by Nelson and Simpson (1994), 17 claimed that false memories were implanted by hypnosis. This is not to impugn the effectiveness of hypnosis as a primary modality or adjunctive therapeutic tool for specific disorders. Our criticism is of hypnosis as a memory recovery tool.

Guided Imagery

Like hypnosis, guided imagery can be an effective technique for helping patients to prepare for stressful events by rehearsing them in their imagination. Some believe that adding tactile, olfactory, visual, and auditory sensations to the imagery increases its generalization to the natural environment. However, our concern is with guided imagery when used as a memory recovery technique. It has been suggested that techniques that allow the survivor to "return" to the original abuse event (e.g., through guided imagery) may replicate enough of the survivor's original affective experience to allow recovery of state-dependent materials. (Briere, 1992, p. 134)

When combined with suggestive instructions and the information that abuse may exist hidden in the memory, patients may create or magnify memories of abuse. To our knowledge, no scientific evidence supports the use of guided imagery as a memory recovery technique.

Journaling

Like hypnosis and guided imagery, journal writing has a long and accepted tradition within psychotherapy of helping patients monitor their thoughts, feelings, and reactions to situations between psychotherapy sessions. Our concern is only with journaling when used as a memory recovery technique. Some psychotherapists have allegedly used free writing or trance writing as a means to recover lost memories of abuse. Again, we have been unable to find any scientific evidence that writing journals while in a trance recovers accurate memories of past events.

Sodium Amytal

Interviews under sodium amytal do not necessarily produce the truth. One of the issues in the *Ramona* case (see chapter 2, this volume) was the nature of the information given to the patient about the effects of sodium amytal. Some expert witnesses in that trial claimed that the patient was told that the information obtained in the sodium amytal interview would be accurate. Others denied any such instruction was given. Both sides concurred that sodium amytal should not be presented as a truth serum, and its limitations should be explained to the patient ahead of time (Cruz-Lat, 1994b).

Premature Interpretation of Memory Fragments

We know of no cases in which malpractice was charged solely on the basis of allegedly premature interpretation or overinterpretation of memory fragments. Nevertheless, we can envision a case in which it is alleged that the psychotherapist magnified or expanded on the significance or details of a memory fragment.

When dealing with memory fragments, psychotherapists should remain neutral and not impose their beliefs or speculations on the patient. "As the therapist listens, she must constantly remind herself to make no assumptions about either the factors or the meaning of the trauma to the patient" (Herman, 1992, p. 179). Memory fragments from an apparently lost trauma are subject to interpretations (or misinterpretations) based on preexisting biases in the therapist. Premature conclusions on the part of the psychotherapist or the patient can alter the subsequent direction of the search. "As the patient accumulates memory traces without contextual biasing, the process of event reconstruction becomes less like a projective test being administered to the therapist" (Byrd, 1994, p. 439).

Age Regression

Evidence suggests that age regression does not help patients recall past events accurately. For example, O'Connell, Shor, and Orne (1970) hypnotized subjects to an earlier age and asked them to recall the names of their school classmates. They recalled more names under hypnosis, but they also produced more inaccurate names. Nash (1987) reviewed age regression studies and concluded that "there is no evidence for the idea that hypnosis enables subjects to accurately reexperience the events of childhood or to return to developmentally previous modes of functioning" (p. 49). Although hypnotized subjects typically act more childlike, so can adequately motivated control subjects. "Hypnotic age regression ... elicits a profoundly believed in experience that may have important diagnostic and therapeutic properties

... but it does not seem to involve a bona fide return to or reinstatement of childhood functioning" (Nash, 1987, p. 50).

Body Work

Some claim that the memories of abuse are stored in the body. For example, Oksana (1994) in a self-help book wrote that

> recent findings indicate that the mind likely resides in the entire person, including the body. There appears to be both memory and intelligence at a cellular level. However, our bodies, unlike our intellect, cannot be manipulated.... The information coming from our bodies is irrefutable. If your body has retained unresolved pain, has scars, or reenacts an event, you can be certain that the pain, the injury, or the event happened. (p. 316)

According to this line of reasoning the trauma has had an impact on the body and reveals itself through muscle tension, labored posture, or other bodily sensations. Moreover, it is argued that massaging the body may evoke memories of past traumas. Goldstein and Farmer (1994) reported on an interview with a psychotherapist who stated,

> When I'm working with someone and their body tells the story and their feelings are so connected with their body—I believe them strongly.... My gut knows truth. I know when someone is bull-shitting—I can feel it. You can't fake feelings really well when they are deep down. It's really hard to fake it because people go back to being children. (p. 197)

However, intense emotions and intuition are not adequate to corroborate past events. There is no evidence that traumas or other psychological difficulties are stored as irrefutably accurate memories in muscles and create discomfort or other bodily sensations. Memories are stored in neurons, not in soft tissues. Although anxious people may have tense muscles, and some people have been classically conditioned to certain stimuli, this does not mean that memories of these events are stored in muscles. Nonetheless, claims of body memories have been made in the self-help literature, and patients and some psychotherapists may believe them.

Other Techniques

Reports have been made of the use of past-life regression therapy, alien abduction therapy, channeling, or exorcisms of devils to retrieve memories of past abuse. These procedures have no legitimate professional support as methods to treat mental illnesses. Practitioners who use these techniques are highly vulnerable to malpractice suits in the event that their patients suffer harm.

Cautions When Using Memory Retrieval Techniques

As should be made clear from this review, the use of memory retrieval techniques places the psychotherapist at legal risk. It would be relatively easy to find expert clinical and scientific witnesses to testify that these techniques cannot be used to retrieve accurate memories and that they could create false memories. For ethical, legal, clinical, and scientific reasons, we recommend against using these special memory retrieval techniques.

Nevertheless, some respected clinicians believe that it is therapeutically indicated, under limited circumstances, to seek to retrieve or "de-repress" memories of abuse through hypnotherapy, sodium amytal interviews, or other means. According to Gold, Hughes, and Hohnecker (1994), Terr (1994), and Herman (1992), these techniques may be justified when the psychotherapists have objective criteria that strongly suggest hidden trauma and the patient has severe suffering. We agree with these practitioners that these techniques are recommended only when more prosaic techniques of memory recovery (talking) have failed and the patients have been informed of the limitations of these techniques and their potential for creating false memories.

If used at all, any memory retrieval technique must be used in the context of the overall treatment of the patient. According to Briere (1992) and Herman (1992), the treatment of adult survivors may fail if psychotherapists fail to focus on the goals of treatment, fail to allow patients time to process whatever memories they do recall, or are too quick to use unproven techniques to recover lost memories. We would also add that some psychotherapists apparently fail to inform patients of the unproven nature of these techniques and fail to document the treatment and memory recovery adequately. We discuss informed consent and documentation in more detail later in this chapter.

Failure to Focus on the Goals of Treatment

Although Gold, Hughes, and Hohnecker (1994) acknowledge that it is sometimes appropriate to attempt to retrieve past memories, they believe that the major focus of treatment should be the "enhancement of functioning and diminution of the post-traumatic effects of abuse rather than the uncovering of abuse memories per se" (p. 441). Retrieving memories alone is not an acceptable treatment plan.

Failure to Process the Memories Adequately

Psychotherapy may not help patients if it only involves the recovery of memories. Instead, patients should be helped to understand the meaning of these memories and how to incorporate them into the perception of themselves and their relationships with their families and others. If psychotherapists do try to help patients recover memories, they should allow patients to approach memories of sexual abuse at their own pace with the psychotherapist maintaining neutrality. Patients may not have the internal resources to handle a flood of unpleasant memories. "Programs that promote the rapid uncovering of traumatic memories without providing an adequate context for integration are therapeutically irresponsible and potentially dangerous for they leave the patient without the resources to cope with the memories uncovered" (Herman, 1992, p. 184).

Although we do not advocate the use of memory retrieval techniques, if they are used the psychotherapist needs to precede each memory retrieval venture with careful preparation and allow for an adequate period of reintegration of the new knowledge. The lack of reintegration was apparent in the case of a former patient who once called one of the authors [S.K.]. She said that she had been feeling depressed and went into psychotherapy. During psychotherapy, she said that she learned that she had been sexually abused as a child ("I wasn't aware of that until I went into psychotherapy"). However, she said that after undergoing hypnosis and having these memories retrieved, she was feeling worse and having continual flashbacks of the abuse. "Am I supposed to feel this way?" she asked.

In the *Ramona* case noted above, an expert witness had testified that the social worker had scheduled the confrontation between the patient and her father only one day after the patient received the sodium amytal treatments that brought to surface the memories of abuse (Cruz-Lat, 1994a). She opined that patients need more time to reflect on the implications of their memory retrieval activities.

Failure to Use More Prosaic Techniques

Another error is to focus on special memory recovery techniques at the expense of the more prosaic but more effective strategy of providing a caring and safe therapeutic environment in which survivors feel empowered to explore their memories. Talking about one's past and current concerns in a safe and supportive environment is consistent with the first rule of psychotherapy: "Do no harm." Reviere (1996) went further and noted that memory work may be contraindicated where there are suspicions of trauma without memory because "suggesting the healing depends on memory recovery may seriously bias the client's own natural process of growth and healing" (p. 109).

The use of memory recovery techniques may appear at first blush to be a convenient way for the unsophisticated psychotherapist to avoid the unpleasant testing of therapeutic boundaries and the ambivalent transference and countertransference feelings that may arise from talk therapy. It may appear to be easier to recover memories, blame a parent or another adult who is not present, and then discharge the patient.

If psychotherapists believe it is necessary to retrieve past memories, then they should avoid promising a quick procedure for uncovering the past, such as a group marathon session or in-patient stay. Rapid memory recovery programs may encourage the creation of memories without concern for their accuracy, and they may fail to give patients enough time to obtain corroborating information or to understand the trauma in the context of their total life experience.

The optimal manner of retrieving past events involves talking with patients, eliciting their feelings, helping them understand the impact of past traumas on their present lives, and teaching them how to make their everyday functioning more productive (Herman, 1992). Even proponents of memory retrieval techniques believe that they are usually not necessary to help patients. "The simplest technique for the recovery of new memories is the careful exploration of memories the patient already has. Most of the time this plain, workaday approach is sufficient" (Herman, 1992, p. 184). Again, if used at all, memory retrieval techniques should be used carefully and selectively.

Other Treatment Procedures

No doubt many patients can benefit from bibliotherapy or group therapy. Care must be taken, however, that the adjuncts to therapy are individually tailored to the needs of the patient. Problems may occur when psychotherapists assign survivor bibliotherapy or survivor group therapy indiscriminately. "Interventions and resources that may be therapeutic at one stage may be ineffective or even destructive at another stage of treatment" (Pope & Brown, 1996, p. 201). Also, the use of reparenting therapy is especially likely to expose psychotherapists to legal difficulties.

Survivor Bibliotherapy

It is very unlikely that a psychotherapist would be held liable only for recommending a particular book. However, the recommendation of a book written specifically for survivors may, along with other actions, imply a diagnosis of childhood abuse or an endorsement of the treatment or memory recovery techniques found in the book. Although these books may benefit some survivors, they may also create harm if used inappropriately. Survivor bibliotherapy and survivor oriented group therapy should be withheld until there is a reasonable degree of certainty about the abuse. The psychotherapist assumes responsibility for discussing the strengths and limitations of recommended books and their application to the patient.

Survivor Groups

Psychotherapists could be held liable for a negligent referral, or referral to groups or practitioners whom they knew, or should have known, were not competent or appropriate for a specific patient. As with survivor bibliotherapy, the decision to refer a patient to a survivor oriented adjunctive therapy group depends on the individual needs of the patient and the nature of the group. "Because of the emotional intensity of the task, the membership of the trauma-focused group must be carefully selected" (Herman, 1992, p. 223).

In some self-help groups, the sharing of memories by some survivors may influence the memories of others who were not certain whether they were abused (Rogers, 1994). Many of the recanters surveyed by Nelson and Simpson (1994) claimed that their group therapy sessions were coercive. One recanter said, "The group progressed from eating disorders to childhood sexual abuse, to incest, to SRA. Eight of the ten members developed SRA memories, the two who didn't were told they were in denial" (p. 126). Because of this potential for "contagion," survivor groups have an inherent limitation as an assessment device to help the patient without memories of abuse retrieve them or as a vehicle to help patients confront their denial.

Furthermore, without professional leaders who have a scientific and professional background and who are trained in professional ethics, self-help groups are vulnerable to developing zealous or grandiose leaders who intrude on other group members. "Some self-help groups remain prone to an exploitative or an oppressive, idiosyncratic group agenda" (Herman, 1992, p. 221). Others become preoccupied with pseudoscience explanations, such as the dedication with which some members of Schizophrenics Anonymous held on to the megavitamin theory of treating schizophrenia (Galanter, 1988).

Intense dependency within the group may discourage persons from completing their treatment goals and graduating from the group. Goldstein and Farmer (1994) report that some patients are told that the group represents their "new family." It may not be harmful for a patient, in a moment of appreciation of the closeness of the group, to refer to the group members as their family. However, the group is not the family of the patient, and groups should not be presented as a desirable alternative to a family of origin. The group members do not have genetic ties, decades-long histories of shared experiences, or life-long commitments to each other. Nor would a family likely discontinue contact with members because they lost the ability to pay for services or their third-party reimbursement ended. Instead, the normal rules found in group psychotherapy, including bans on out-of-session socialization, should apply. The group psychotherapist is not a parent, but a professional who has the responsibility to model clear boundaries and monitor the behavior of other members (Donaldson & Cordes-Green, 1994).

Reparenting

During reparenting the psychotherapist reenacts the parental role with the patient. Supposedly, patients will receive the nurturing they lacked as children and will be able to experience their infancy again without any of the trauma involved. McNamara (1994) described the case of a woman who sued her psychiatrist for using this technique. "His attempts to 'reparent' his patient included having her suck his thumb, suck his breast nipples, nurse a baby bottle, and wear diapers" (p. 45). In a newspaper report reprinted in the *FMS Foundation Newsletter*, Poor (1995) described a case in which one therapist team allegedly convinced their patient that she needed to be reparented. The patient's parents "claim that ... [the husband and wife therapy team] encouraged Linda [the patient] to call them 'mom and dad,' and to terminate her relationship with her biological parents" (p. 13). We have been unable to find any outcome studies using reparenting. In our view, reparenting is therapeutically contraindicated and legally risky.

Obtain Informed Consent
(Patient Participation)

We believe that psychotherapy is most effective when patients are involved in the decision-making process regarding their therapy. Patient participation in the treatment process has been called informed consent by many scholars. The very term "informed consent" may be misleading because it implies that the patient is passively consenting to something presented by the psychotherapist. Optimally, the patient and psychotherapist are collaborating to identify and reach mutually agreed-upon goals. Nevertheless, for purposes of this discussion, we will use the traditional term, informed consent.

According to the code of ethics of the APA (1992),

> Psychologists make reasonable efforts to answer patients' questions and to avoid apparent misunderstandings about therapy. Whenever possible, psychologists provide oral and/or written information, using language that is reasonably understandable to the patient or client.

Standard 4.01d) [and] Psychologists obtain appropriate informed consent to therapy or related procedures, using language that is reasonably understandable to participants. The content of informed consent will vary depending on many circumstances; however, informed consent generally implies that the person (1) has the capacity to consent, (2) has been informed of significant information concerning the procedure, (3) has freely and without undue influence expressed consent, and (4) consent has been appropriately documented. (Standard 4.01d and 4.02a)

Elements of Informed Consent

The nature and scope of the information that the psychotherapist should provide to the patient about therapeutic techniques vary according to the sophistication and needs of the patient. A general rule for the psychotherapist is to ask what the average person would want to know about the procedure. Previous courts dealing with informed consent have ruled that patients should have the opportunity to learn the risks and benefits of treatment procedures. According to *Canterbury v. Spence* (1972),

> Physician has duty as part of due care, to warn of danger lurking in proposed treatment and to impart information which patient has every right to expect; reasonable explanation required means generally informing patient in nontechnical terms as to what is at stake, i.e. the therapy alternatives open to him, goals expected or believed to be achieved, and risks which may ensue from particular treatment and no treatment. (p. 773)

However, in *Cobb v. Grant* (1972), the court clarified, "Patient's interest in medical information does not extend to lengthy polysyllabic discourse on all possible complications; [a] minicourse in medical science is not required" (p. 2).

Elements that should be included in the informed consent process include statements about the general nature of therapy, the role of the memory retrieval techniques (if used at all) as a way to meet the overall goals of therapy, and an explanation of the benefits and risks of those procedures (Nagy, 1994).

Informed Consent with Unproven Techniques

Patients need to be aware of the inherent dangers of unproven therapeutic techniques. Memory recovery techniques have not yet proven their accuracy in retrieving childhood events, or their efficacy in improving daily functioning or treating disorders (or their potential for creating false memories). Unless patients have been advised of their limitations, the use of memory retrieval techniques will be difficult to support in the event of litigation. Even if patients have been advised of their limitations, their mere use for memory retrieval may subject the psychotherapist to criticism. This does not necessarily mean that these techniques should be avoided altogether because they may be used for purposes other than memory retrieval such as to identify affect or as a projective technique.

Some writers have suggested that it is a good practice to provide patients with brochures that describe therapeutic techniques. A brief printed brochure on the memory retrieval procedure might help reinforce what the patient is told verbally. The brochure could indicate the limitations to and benefits of the memory retrieval technique. If a brochure is used, care must be taken that it does not guarantee results, create unrealistic expectations, or minimize the risk of creating false memories. A potential risk of providing a brochure about a technique is that it may make the technique look more important and established than it really is.

The informed consent form should be used to supplement, not replace, reasoned conversations between the psychotherapist and the patient. Consent is an ongoing process that involves dialogue and responses to questions that emerge as the treatment progresses. The informed consent form only documents and reinforces those conversations. Signing an informed consent form is, in and of itself, meaningless unless it is done in the context of discussion and understanding on the part of the patient. A sample patient participation (informed consent) form is presented in Appendix C. Pope and Brown (1996) also provide helpful information on informed consent.

Informed Consent and Hypnosis

We reiterate that we have no criticism with the use of hypnosis for the treatment of particular problems; the concern is with hypnosis as a memory recovery technique. Although the psychotherapist may not intend to use hypnosis in an inappropriate way, care must be taken that the patient does not misinterpret the purpose of hypnosis. Great care must be taken in presenting it to the patient.

The American Society of Clinical Hypnosis has provided a sample consent form for using hypnosis (Hammond et al., 1994, pp. 48–49). We also recommend that psychotherapists who consider using hypnosis with adult survivors of abuse carefully review the book entitled, *Clinical Hypnosis and Memory: Guidelines for Clinicians and for Forensic Hypnosis*, published by the American Society of Clinical Hypnosis (Hammond et al., 1994).

For example, therapists need to explain carefully to the patient that hypnosis is not a truth serum. It may enhance the retrieval of accurate memories, but it also increases the recall of inaccurate memories. A review of the memory enhancing effects of hypnosis shows that it has no unique ability to retrieve memories. Rather, the intense effort at memory retrieval appears responsible for any enhanced memory recall that may occur. Furthermore, hypnosis can lead to concreting or increasing the confidence that participants have in their reported beliefs, even though they lack empirical support for their increased confidence (Spanos, Burgess, & Burgess, 1994).

Hammond (1995) also adds that it is prudent for hypnotists to solicit the patients' expectations of what benefit they will receive from the hypnotic procedure. This will elicit beliefs that may have to be corrected before hypnosis can proceed. Furthermore, in order to reduce the suggestibility of the hypnotic procedure, Hammond recommends that patients be told that they should not regard the questions they are asked as suggestions and that it is appropriate to answer "I don't know" to any question. Bloom (1994) suggests some language to give patients when embarking on hypnosis:

> There is no guarantee that what you experience in hypnosis actually happened. Sometimes hypnotic recollections have no more to do with historical events than do dreams. Automatically accepting the events of a hypnotic reverie as directly representing historical fact would be as unfortunate as accepting the events of a dream as literal representations of past events. Much as with a dream, what you experience in hypnosis can undoubtedly be exceedingly important, but that does not mean that it is accurate. (p. 176)

When discussing the data derived from memory recovery therapy, it is prudent for psychotherapists to refer to them as "impressions," "sensations," "experiences," or similar terms that reflect the tentative nature of the recollections. Referring to the recollections as "facts" may mislead the patient into believing that the information recalled is accurate (Nagy, 1994).

Finally, patients should be informed that the fact that the memories were retrieved through hypnosis may preclude their acceptability to a court in the event that litigation is contemplated (see Appendix E for comments about hypnosis included in the statement by the APA Working Group on Investigation of Memories of Childhood Abuse).

Show Concern for Family Relationships

As noted in the section on patient relationships, it can be considered a boundary violation to encourage patients to go public with their concerns by confronting family members or to encourage patients to sue their alleged perpetrators. According to the Australian Psychological Society (1994), "psychologists should recognize that their responsibilities are to the therapeutic needs of clients, and not to issues of legal action or revenge" (p. 4). Few authors encourage such confrontations. Even Bass and Davis, among some of the strongest proponents of identifying repressed childhood abuse, stated that "confrontations are not essential to healing. The choice to confront is a personal one" (1994, p. 340).

Several legal considerations are also relevant here. Although only one court has held that a duty exists between psychotherapists and the parents of adult children, additional suits alleging such harm may be filed in the future. In addition, suits could still be pursued by the accused family member on the basis of defamation or by the former patient on the basis of traditional negligence. The legal risks associated with confrontations are much less when the therapist is acting as a mediator.

Family Confrontations

According to Poole et al. (1995), about 27% of patients who recovered memories of abuse during psychotherapy eventually confronted their abusers and 37% terminated relations with their abusers. Lief and Fetkewicz (1995) reported that 27 of 40 recanters reported that their psychotherapists had told them not to communicate with their family members.

An accusation of child abuse may create lifelong anger and alienation among family members. The psychotherapist and patient should consider the motive for the family confrontation. They should ask themselves whether revenge or blame will promote the long-term personal growth and happiness of the patient. Although Herman (1992) believes that family confrontations can be therapeutic and empowering, she noted that they are not without problems. Traditional family dynamics of dominance and submission may make the confrontation difficult; some family members may deny the events or become alienated from the accuser. Mediation, an alternative to confrontation, is discussed later in this chapter.

Some psychotherapists appear to minimize the harm and consequences that can come from accusations of abuse. For example, Fredrickson (1992) told readers that they should not be overly concerned about making a false accusation of abuse. She stated that for victims "this need for justice can take on an exaggerated importance" because the abused patient has "become too sensitive to fairness issues" (p. 160). She also stated that patients need not try to get external corroboration of the abuse. Strong feelings of denial on the part of the victim toward a possible past perpetrator are also suspect. "Such strong feelings are sometimes more of an indication of a hated truth than a false accusation" (p. 186).

Fredrickson (1992) also advised patients who confront abusers to maintain their conviction about the abuse and their decision to confront even when abusers deny that the abuse happened. Fredrickson (1992) wrote,

> Sometimes there is outrage, but usually the abuser will be cool and collected, simply stating that there is no truth to what you are saying. This calm attitude can be very influential to other family members who do not want to believe you in the first place. Do not retreat. You may want to suggest that the abuser has repressed all memory of the abuse. (p. 206)

Although psychotherapists have a primary responsibility for their patients, psychotherapists should not be oblivious to the consequences for others. The aspirational section of the APA code of ethics (1992) states that

> in their professional actions, psychologists weigh the welfare and rights of their patients or clients, students, supervisees, human research participants, and other affected persons ... (Principle E)

A high threshold should be required before a memory fragment or an inkling is turned into a belief. When patients without a clear memory of abuse want to go public with their accusations, they should consider asking for impartial sources of verification such as hospital or physician records, recollections of other family members, or other sources. According to Terr (1994), patients seldom fabricate completely false stories of abuse. Instead, "parts are true—often the gist. Parts are false—sometimes the details in the descriptions of the perpetrators" (p. 203). Inaccuracy in identifying the perpetrators is especially common when the patient has massive dissociation or splitting (Terr, 1994).

It is possible for patients to misconstrue certain therapeutic techniques as encouraging confrontations or detachment. For example, Paddison, Einbinder, Maker, and Strain (1993) described a treatment exercise in which group therapy members write a letter to the perpetrator or nonoffending parent "to get in touch with feelings about the incest and as a way to empower their ability to be heard" (p. 41). Although the letter was not necessarily written to be sent, the very exercise of writing the letter could be construed as endorsing or encouraging a public confrontation. Pendergast (1995) described a patient who developed an accusing letter on the advice of her psychotherapist, but was astonished when the psychotherapist chastised her for actually sending the letter.

Unfortunately, some psychotherapists appear to believe that they have a social responsibility to encourage confrontations with alleged perpetrators out of a concern for the "silent victims" who are afraid to come forth. However, the encouragement of confrontations risks a boundary violation in which the therapist's allegiance shifts from the patient to nonpatients. Although it is highly desirable for all persons to work to reduce childhood abuse, using the dependence engendered in psychotherapy to enlist a patient to help redress this social wrong violates appropriate boundaries.

Detachment

As with the decision to seek a family confrontation, it is the patient's decision whether or not to detach from the perpetrator. The role of the psychotherapist should be to help the patient consider the possible consequences. Psychotherapists should help patients clarify their goals in light of their unique life circumstances.

Family Litigation

Poole et al. (1995) found that about 6% of the victims who recovered memories of lost abuse took legal actions against their alleged abusers. Pope and Tabachnick (1995) found that 12% of female patients and 5% of male patients who recovered lost memories of abuse filed a civil or criminal complaint against their alleged abusers. Clute (1993), an attorney, claims that litigation can be a positive healing experience for some patients. She wrote,

> ... When adult survivor litigation is approached as an integral part of the therapeutic process, through the concerted efforts of the survivor, the attorney and the therapist working together, the success may be measured on a scale beyond the dollars won and recovery may be achieved on a level not otherwise possible. (p. 127)

Litigation against family members is an option chosen by some survivors of childhood abuse. However, litigation may exacerbate symptoms, in part, because patients lose their traditional support systems (McNulty & Wardle, 1994). Even Clute (1993) acknowledges the likely disruption in family relationships. She stated,

> Another unique but inevitable development in some cases is that the client's decision to pursue litigation will be a decision to be rejected by most, if not all, of one's birth family. The attorney and treating therapist may be among few to share this life-changing event with the adult survivor. Becoming a member of the survivor's replacement family on some level is a likely result, a commitment that some will accept but many may find threatening. (p. 127)

Bass and Davis (1994) noted that survivors should not undertake lawsuits with the intent of getting the abuser to admit what he or she has done. They also acknowledge the emotional drain involved in lawsuits as unpleasant memories of the past are revisited. "It is notoriously slow, frustrating, grueling, and often expensive. Although the outcome may be worth the work and stress, the toll a lawsuit takes should not be underestimated" (p. 318).

Rosen (1995) found that survivors of a maritime disaster who filed lawsuits reported far more PTSD (posttraumatic stress disorder) symptoms than has been found among survivors of similar maritime disasters. Although the study had some methodological problems, it raises the possibility that the process of litigation itself, if it involves symptom sharing, inadvertent symptom prompting by attorneys, or secondary gains, may exacerbate PTSD symptoms. Similar effects may occur among victims who have suffered from childhood abuse. The very process of litigation may inadvertently and unconsciously encourage them to worsen their symptoms. It would be an even greater tragedy if the accusation were to be made solely on the basis of memories that were recovered through interventions that have not yet been proven effective in retrieving accurate memories and that have been proven to create inaccurate memories in some patients.

When considered only from a psychotherapeutic perspective, the decision to initiate lawsuits is often contraindicated. The very process of litigation forces patients to increase the emphasis on their symptoms and pain. It diverts them from their therapeutic task of getting on with their lives and assuming responsibility for their own welfare. Patients may spend years in expensive litigation with numerous appeals and delays and receive a hollow victory whereby, even if they win, they have lost their families (London, 1995). Patients with credible or verified stories of abuse who receive legal advice that they have a good chance of winning their case may decide to sue in an effort to win money from their perpetrators. Guthiel (1995) concludes that patients should not expect psychological satisfaction or gains (validation) from these lawsuits.

Our review of this literature suggests that some patients do gain a sense of satisfaction and justice, but for others litigation may be contraindicated. Psychotherapists should assist their patients in weighing the benefits and risks of litigation to their mental health. Psychotherapists should avoid pressuring their patients to sue.

Mediation

Alternative dispute resolution mechanisms may be a more appropriate recourse for many patients. These techniques allow the children and their parents to discuss their perceptions, gain a common ground, identify possible areas of disagreements, and consider what their relationship will be from here on. Mediation reduces hostility, in part, because discussions are not in the courtroom where proceedings are adversarial by their very nature. Room is available for give and take and to admit mistakes without disastrous repercussions. It allows for healing and honest discussion. The willingness to spend time with a family member to heal the wounds, despite its inherent discomfort, is often perceived as a healing act in and of itself.

The family mediation process recognizes that it may be impossible to accurately reconstruct some past family events. The task of helping patients recall childhood events is daunting. Children have difficulty evaluating the social meaning and context of events that are ambiguous to them. Small children may have difficulty understanding when washing their genitals is normal bathing and when it is abusive. In one example, an adult may report that as a child she was required to perform erotic dances in front of her father wearing only a bathing suit. The parent may recall a family picnic when the child danced spontaneously to music after coming back from the lake where they were swimming. Although the essential fact that the child danced in her bathing suit was not disputed, the context and the meaning of the event was. Given the uncertainty surrounding the recollection of some events, it may be difficult for some adult children to have absolute certainty about events when confronting their parents. Mediation recognizes this inherent difficulty with memories.

Of course, mediation is not an option in all cases as one or more of the parties may be too angry, resistive, deceptive, or defensive for it to succeed. Or, the patients may decide that they do not wish to rebuild their relationships with the alleged perpetrators. In addition, the mediation process may, if not conducted properly, be unfair to one of the parties. For example, the mediator may not be neutral or may lead one of the parties to agree to "split the difference" (acquiesce to "truths" solely to keep the process going).

Risk Management and Confrontations

Citing risk management reasons, Caudill (1995) urges psychotherapists who treat adult survivors of childhood abuse to refrain from family confrontations as part of therapy. The very fact of bringing a parent into a therapy session, he says, could be interpreted by some courts as establishing a psychotherapist–patient relationship with the allegedly abusing parent and thus providing the aggrieved parent with a legal basis for suing the psychotherapist for malpractice. Furthermore, Caudill notes that psychotherapists who participate or encourage confrontations with parents need to understand their inherent bias. These psychotherapists have received information from only one person. Their therapeutic relationship may prevent them from acting objectively to understand the truth, regardless of the perceptions of their patients. He suggests that confrontations, if any, should not be managed by the treating psychotherapists.

As noted previously, in *Khatian v. Jones* (1994) a psychiatrist was sued for slander on the basis of remarks he made during a family session. The manner and details of the confrontation made a suit likely. The memory was retrieved through the use of sodium amytal, which is an unreliable memory recovery technique, and the patient had recanted the accusation of abuse before the family session began. Furthermore, the psychiatrist presented the accusations as facts, instead of as perceptions or allegations.

Even when patients have a more credible memory of abuse, the abuse should not be mentioned at all unless it is related to the treatment goals for the patient. Even in those circumstances, the psychotherapist should make it clear that the accusation is based on the descriptions of the patient and not from any special expertise or technique on the part of the psychotherapist.

Building a Healthy Skepticism

The Role of the Psychotherapist

The role of psychotherapists is to help patients make decisions about their lives, including decisions about confronting or suing perpetrators. A distinction needs to be made between the role of the psychologist as a psychotherapist and as a forensic evaluator. The role of the forensic evaluator is to assist the courts by providing information about the patient relevant to the issues before the court. Whereas the psychologist as psychotherapist can focus on the memory impressions and subjective meaning developed by the patient, the psychologist as forensic evaluator must be concerned with the relationship of these impressions and meanings to the legal issues before the court. As psychotherapists help patients make decisions about legal issues, the psychologist should show concern for the patients' future relationships with their families. It is not always ethical for a psychotherapist to say, "I only respond to what my patient says, I do not concern myself with the objective accuracy of her report." If the patient intends to confront, detach, or to initiate a lawsuit against her parents, then she deserves the benefit of an informed opinion concerning the veracity of her perceptions or the scientific basis of the techniques used to retrieve her memories. Although it may please patients if their psychotherapists believe (or act like they believe) their accounts, they need to know that the criminal and civil courts will adopt a higher and more objective standard of truth.

As detailed in sections above, memories retrieved through memory recovery techniques can be easily challenged in court. On the other hand, a patient who always had a clear memory of abuse would be a much more credible plaintiff. Also, the likely accuracy of the perceived memory probably decreases as the bizarre nature of the accusations, in the absence of corroborating evidence, increases. A higher threshold of skepticism should occur when patients retrieve memories of abuse that occurred at a very early age, involved satanic rituals, or occurred under other highly unusual circumstances.

Infant Amnesia

A psychotherapist who is aware of the phenomenon of childhood amnesia would have reservations about accepting the validity of a recollection of an event that, for example, occurred before the child reached the age of 2 and certainly before the age of 1. Everyone suffers from *infant amnesia* or the inability to reliably recall experiences from the first years of life. Most people's earliest memories are of after they were 3 years old. Only a few can recall events before the age of 1. Of course, some "remembered" events may be reconstructions based on descriptions given by parents, siblings, or other witnesses. Some psychotherapists have allegedly helped patients recall *preverbal memories*. Patients report recalling that their fathers abused them in the crib, or even before 6 months of age (Pendergast, 1995). A survey by the False Memory Syndrome Foundation in the United States showed that 35% of the accusing children reported uncovering memories of abuse that occurred before the age of 2 and 68% before the age of 4 (Freyd, in press). However, the survey asked when the abuse first began. It is possible that the patient accurately remembered later events, although the veracity of the early events remains more questionable. Nevertheless, these reports suggest that patients are either entering therapy with preconceived notions of very early childhood memories or are acquiring those memories during psychotherapy.

A distinction needs to be made between adult memories of childhood abuse and childhood behavior that may suggest abuse. Although adults do not have reliable memories of early events, children may have reactions to early abuse, even though they cannot verbally describe the abuse. For example, a child survivor of sexual abuse that occurred before she was 2 years old, was noted to frequently draw pictures of naked men and women. The allegations of her abuse were later supported by the confiscation of child pornography materials by police. Some might argue that the child's drawings were a diagnostic manifestation of the abuse. Another way to understand the child's drawings, however, is to consider that the sexualized drawings might be a product of attitudes, behaviors, and observations of adults around the child who condoned or took pornographic pictures. In such an atmosphere, a child might be expected to demonstrate inappropriate sexual attitudes and behaviors. Unfortunately, no behavioral or psychological childhood signs reliably indicate childhood abuse. The large majority of victims of child abuse after the age of 3 or 4 remember the abuse. However, Lindsay and Read (1995) believe that victims may avoid thinking about it because it is painful or they may be reluctant to talk about it unless they are in a safe and secure environment.

Satanic Ritualistic Abuse

In addition to ordinary child abuse, concerns have been raised about the frequency of allegations of satanic ritualistic abuse (SRA). Between 17% and 18% of the parents who contacted the FMS Foundation reported that they had been accused of SRA (Accusations, 1993; Family Survey Update, 1994).

Some religious, ritualistic, or satanic abuse does occur. One of the authors [S.K.] had one young girl as a patient who was sexually abused as part of the religious rites of her parents' nature-worshipping religion, although it was not apparently a witch or satanic based church. The case was well documented by the courts; the girl was under custody of Children and Youth Services, and some of the perpetrators were imprisoned for the offenses against her and other children. Apparently they defended themselves in court on the basis of freedom of religion, as opposed to denying the offenses.

A small number of satanists and witches quietly practice their religion and some do include sexual activities in their rituals. Adherents of witchcraft vary considerably in their ritual practices. Some only include private consensual sexual practices between adults in their ceremonies. Others allow children to watch their ceremonies. Still others include painful or coerced sexual practices. Some Satan worshippers have complained that child molesters are joining satanic churches or using the trappings of satanic worship as a pretext for child abuse (Parker, 1993).

However, suggestions of satanic worship also occur when some youths adopt an occasional symbol or ritual of satanism as part of their rebellion against authority. Their involvement most often reflects a superficial adoption of rituals without any adherence to a satanic worldview or an involvement with a committed coterie of satanists. Also, a few patients with serious mental illness may adopt satanic explanations and incorporate them into their delusional or hallucinatory systems. Finally, other reports of satanic ritualistic abuse may reflect sexual behavior that is more sadistic than satanic per se. Much sadistic sexual behavior is ritualistic and involves common practices that are eroticized for the abuser such as binding the victims, inflicting pain during the process of sexual activity, and making the victims wear chains, bonds, or eroticized clothing.

Nevertheless, false memories probably account for many reports of SRA, which have become increasingly incredible. There are suggestions that satanists have killed hundreds (perhaps thousands) of persons and have routinely engaged in the ritualistic torture and murder of hundreds of children and adults. According to Pendergast (1995), patients have alleged that they were impregnated at the age of 9, or forced to kill, mutilate, or eat ritually killed victims. Ross (1994) reports allegations of having a fetus fed to a dog, killing an old woman and burying her in the backyard, and seeing one's grandmother fly on a broom. Survivors of satanic cults have become popular on the talk show circuit. However, direct evidence of these activities is lacking, and extensive criminal investigations have failed to yield solid evidence of widespread satanic activities or conspiracies (Lanning, 1992).

Furthermore, these findings are consistent with the theory

that the identification of satanic ritualistic abuse appears to depend more on the perspective of the treating psychotherapist than on the objective circumstances of the patient. McMinn and Wade (1995) found that psychologists who were members of the American Association of Christian Counselors were more likely to treat patients with SRA than a random sample of counseling psychologists from APA Division 17 (Counseling Psychology). Nevertheless, both groups reported very low rates of SRA among their patients (1.6% for the Christian Counselors sample and .03% for the Division 17 sample). According to Bottoms (as cited in Schneider, 1994) whereas about one third of psychotherapists reported that they have treated at least one patient alleging satanic or religiously motivated abuse, a very few psychotherapists report treating dozens or even hundreds of cases. Poole et al. (1995) reported that the top 5% of clinicians were responsible for 58% of the reports of treating patients who claimed to be victims of satanic abuse. Of course, not all clinicians believed all the reports of abuse.

Coons' study (1994) of SRA cases in a dissociative disorders clinic shows the potential influence of suggestion on the development of SRA beliefs on the part of patients. Of 29 patients who entered the clinic between 1984 and 1993 and reported SRA, 17 came forward within 2 years after a Geraldo Rivera show on SRA and 10 came forward 1 year after a local workshop on SRA. In other words, 92% entered the program after one of these two media events. Furthermore, only 2 of the 29 patients came in with memories that were not elicited through memory recovery techniques (hypnosis, dream work, or regressive therapy). Despite efforts to corroborate the reports, no confirmatory evidence of SRA was found for any of the patients.

Although some reports of satanic ritual abuse likely are true, skepticism must be given to reports in the absence of corroborating evidence, especially if patients are considering confronting or detaching themselves from their family of origin based on those beliefs. For example, one adult child accused her parents of using her as a "breeder" (impregnating her to obtain babies to kill in sacrificial rituals) in her early adolescence. However, the parents obtained a physician's report that she was a virgin at the age of 19 (Goldstein & Farmer, 1994). In another case in which the psychiatrist was successfully sued, the patient claimed that she was bred for babies who were born through Cesarean section; however, she had no Cesarean scar. In another case a young woman claimed that she had been impregnated by her father twice and had been forced to perform a coat-hanger abortion on herself. However, the *FMS Foundation Newsletter* ("Parents, Siblings Join Retractor in Lawsuit," 1996) reported that a gynecologist who examined her found that she was a virgin and her father had had a vasectomy when his daughter was four years old.

Conclusion

Conducting good psychotherapy requires skill and acumen under the best of circumstances. The challenges to the psychotherapist increase when patients believe that they may have been abused or traumatized in the past. In these situations psychologists need to focus on the goals of treatment and lean on their professionally and scientifically derived standards to provide quality services.

6

Documentation, Consultation, and Supervision

Patient records have several purposes. They are a way for psychotherapists to monitor the quality of their treatment, to recall important patient details, to provide for continuity of treatment in the event that the patient receives services from another provider, to justify treatment to third-party payers, and to protect the psychotherapists in the event of an allegation of negligence. A well-written document recording treatment decisions and procedures is a powerful defense against any accusation of negligence. An axiom among malpractice defense attorneys is, "If it isn't written down, it didn't occur" (VandeCreek & Knapp, 1997).

As has been described previously, psychotherapists will not be liable if their patients only suffered harm as a result of psychotherapy. Instead, liability is found if the level of treatment fell below minimally acceptable levels and caused the harm. Good documentation can provide very strong evidence that adequate treatment was provided. In this chapter we review the essential ingredients that should be included in the records of every patient, special situations in which more intense documentation is prudent, and ways to write records so that they more carefully reflect the content of the psychotherapy sessions.

The Use of Routine Documentation

As has been discussed in preceding chapters, the treatment of some patients (such as those who always remembered the abuse in the past) present average legal or ethical risks. For most of these patients, routine documentation is sufficient. As with all patients, psychotherapists should record the presenting problem or diagnosis, the methods used to obtain the diagnosis, the treatment recommended and its relationship to the presenting problem or diagnosis, the substance of each treatment session and any modifications of the treatment plan or diagnosis, and all consultations.

Although the fact of having been abused as a child is not a diagnosis, the psychotherapist should include in the record information about relational or historical factors relevant to treatment. The diagnosis should correspond to the *DSM-IV* (American Psychiatric Association, 1994) criteria or other professionally derived nosology. Because of confidentiality concerns, some psychotherapists are loathe to place information about past abuse in the patient's record. This decision requires clinical judgment on the part of psychotherapists. The patient chart should contain all information that is relevant to the diagnosis and treatment plan and should not be cluttered with extraneous and embarrassing information about the patient.

If, in the opinion of the treating psychotherapist, the abuse appears related to the patient's presenting problems, then it should be documented. Recall of more details as therapy progresses should be noted as well. Often patients enter therapy with memory fragments of abuse. The therapy notes should reflect the initial memory fragment and the patient's increase in recall of the events, if any. If, in the opinion of the psychotherapist, the abuse is incidental or not related to the presenting problem, it need not be recorded in detail (or at all). Of course, the initial impression of the psychotherapist concerning the relative importance of the past abuse may change over the course of therapy. Psychotherapists should increase or decrease their documentation of details of the abuse and its present impact on the patient as the demands of psychotherapy unfold.

Use of Unproven Techniques

The use of techniques for memory retrieval that have no scientific or professional basis (e.g., hypnosis, guided imagery, or journaling to de-repress memory) has inherent clinical and legal risks associated with it. Although we do not recommend these techniques for memory retrieval, we recognize that some competent psychotherapists use them with some patients under limited circumstances. If psychotherapists decide to use specialized techniques to retrieve memory, they should record how the memory retrieval techniques were related to the goals of treatment, that more prosaic memory recovery techniques had failed to be helpful, that the memory recovery techniques were not conducted in such a way as to create or suggest abuse, that the patient was informed of the limitations and risks of these techniques ahead of time, and, if memories were recovered, that they were processed through psychotherapy.

Documentation of what the patient said before, during, and after the memory retrieval session or sessions is indicated. Terr (1994) noted that because it is important to minimize the possibility that therapist bias could influence the content of the memory, contextual cues should be kept as neutral as possible. A videotape or audiotape of the de-repression session can help diffuse possible future accusations of suggestive questioning or misleading contextual cues. This information should be considered part of the patient's record and should be protected and preserved with just as much care as written records.

Psychotherapists should document the informed consent of their patients before any unproven procedures are used. The informed consent procedures should include relevant information on the advantages and disadvantages of the therapeutic techniques, their limitations in retrieving accurate memories, and possible side effects of creating false memories. A handout on the limitations to, and the therapeutic context of, memory retrieval techniques may supplement the information given verbally to the patient. A copy of the handout should be placed in the patient's file. As was discussed earlier, informed consent involves more than just having the patient sign a form. Informed consent requires continual patient involvement in the treatment decisions. Psychotherapists who use unproven techniques should adopt a higher standard of documenting discussions of the use of these unproven techniques.

If the patient decides to detach from, confront, or sue his or her family, then psychotherapists should record their neutrality in helping the patient reach these decisions. The treatment notes should reflect that the psychotherapist helped the patient clarify feelings and thoughts about such a confrontation and the consideration of its eventual outcome. It is especially important for psychotherapists to document that they discussed with the patient the negative aspects of the detachment from, confrontation of, or suit against the alleged perpetrator.

Complex Patient Symptomatology

Psychotherapists should increase their level of documentation as the patient demonstrates increasingly problematic behaviors or complex symptomatology. Some patients demonstrate life-threatening behaviors or ideation. Often psychotherapists will encounter patients who present bizarre and increasingly incredible stories of abuse. Other patients may enter psychotherapy with an intense interest or demand to have past memory fragments verified. Still other patients may become excessively demanding on the time and attention of the psychotherapist and attempt to intrude into the psychotherapist's private life through requests to become friends or through trumped-up emergencies that are an excuse to make many between-session phone calls.

As these behaviors increase, the need for good documentation increases. Patients may feel angered and betrayed by the psychotherapist who fails to believe their incredible stories, who denies the ability to retrieve past memories with complete accuracy, or who insists on appropriate psycho-therapeutic boundaries. Although the professional behavior of the psychotherapist may be faultless, angry patients have been known to file ethics charges based totally on falsehoods. Accurate and detailed notes makes the defense much easier.

For example, in one case a seriously depressed young man in a psychiatric hospital told the attending psychiatrist that he (the patient) had developed a sexual relationship with his previous therapist, also a psychiatrist, and that the previous psychiatrist had told him not to take the medication prescribed for him in the hospital. Maltsberger (1993) reported that the original psychiatrist, however, had notes documenting the psychotic transference of the patient toward her and her continual pleas for him to take the medication as prescribed.

Obtain Past Records

Another problematic behavior is for patients to refuse to allow the release of previous treatment records. Reviewing past records is usually necessary to develop an accurate treatment plan and is a good risk management strategy (Soisson, VandeCreek, & Knapp, 1987). However, sometimes patients will present seemingly good reasons, such as past abuse on the part of the previous psychotherapist or highly insensitive or incompetent treatment. At times these reports may be accurate, but they may also represent falsehoods designed by the patient to hide an accurate report of past manipulative behaviors.

Reports by patients of past misconduct by previous psychotherapists should not be a barrier for attempting to retrieve the records. Even if the reports of abuse are accurate, the records of previous psychotherapists may still contain some useful clinical information. Courts have sometimes concluded that prior records are an essential part of formulating a proper diagnosis and treatment plan. For example, in *Jablonski v. United States* (1983), the court held that the treating psychiatrist "should have known" that his patient had a history of violence toward his lovers. The psychiatrist had failed to obtain prior treatment records that had described the patient's history of violence

Precision In Patient Records

As noted above, some psychotherapists are reluctant to place details in their treatment notes because they fear that a managed care company or another third party may use the notes against the patient. These concerns have some merit, but they should not deter psychotherapists from keeping accurate and comprehensive reports. Most of the possible damage from the disclosure of therapy notes can be avoided if psychologists write their notes carefully. Notes should contain precise behavioral descriptions of symptoms and should not include musings or ill-considered speculations by the psychotherapist. Tentative or working hypotheses should be labeled as such in the notes.

Table 3 contrasts adequate with inadequate notes, which include only broad conclusions on the part of the therapist. The adequate note counterpart includes more precise language and more detail. The source of statements is often identified ("the patient said ..."), jargon such as "low self-esteem" or "codependence" are explained in detail, and relevant quotes are given when appropriate.

Writing in precise language by using behavioral descriptions may appear stilted for some psychotherapists who have been used to writing more jargon-filled notes. Nevertheless, the precise method of writing can become natural and easy with practice and will more accurately describe the patient's clinical picture.

Using Consultation and Supervision Properly

A distinction needs to be made between consultation and supervision as used here. During consultation, the psychotherapist retains the authority to accept or reject the opinion of the consultant because the psychotherapist is qualified and licensed to practice independently. In supervision, however,

Table 3

Adequate and Inadequate Notes

Inadequate Notes	Adequate Notes
She was victimized by her uncle.	The patient reported being victimized by her uncle.
She has low self-esteem.	She remarked that she felt inadequate in her job and like a failure, now that her romance with Bob has ended.
She is codependent.	She expressed dissatisfaction with her relationship with Bob.
	"I tried to hide his drinking from his parents. They never knew how bad it was."
She has all of the signs of a survivor of child abuse.	She presents her problem as low self-esteem and being overly dependent on men.
She is diagnosed as a survivor of child abuse.	Her primary diagnosis is adjustment disorder with depressed mood. She has had poor appetite, trouble sleeping, and self-critical attitudes, which emerged shortly after her romantic breakup.

as defined in this context, the supervisee has no independent authority to treat the patient, and the supervisor retains ultimate authority over the patient's care. Such supervisory arrangements are commonly found with recent graduates who are receiving supervised experience before they are allowed to sit for the licensing examination of their profession. Other examples of this arrangement are psychiatric residents, unlicensed employees of licensed professionals, or psychotherapists who work in institutions or agencies.

Consultation

Practitioners, even if they are licensed and legally able to provide services independently, should consult with other psychotherapists as part of the larger process of self-monitoring and self-improvement of their professional behavior. Self-monitoring could include the use of outcome measures or patient satisfaction reports, a planned continuing education program, or continual contact with other professionals about the quality of diagnostic and treatment techniques.

Consultation is a very effective risk management procedure. As noted several times above, psychotherapists will be evaluated according to the extent to which they adhere to the standards of their profession. Seeking consultation helps ensure that they are providing good treatment to their patients. There is some indication (Polusny & Follette, 1996) that psychologists are more frequently seeking consultation when treating adult patients suspected of being sexually abused as children.

Routine consultations. Consultation should be ongoing for all clinicians. *Peer consultation* or *mutual consultation* groups are an effective way to share information about treatment plans and methods with patients. These groups allow for emotional support and professional feedback for clinicians who are, by the very nature of their profession, engaged in demanding and potentially isolating work.

Peer consultation groups usually work best with 5 to 8 members of comparable educational and experiential background. There should be some general guidelines about protocol within the meeting, such as alternating group leaders or case presentations. Support for each member should be bidirectional. That is, members should be able to give as much as they are able to receive. Groups whose members are unequal in experience may risk having members with greater expertise end up in the role of permanent givers, whereas members with less expertise may end up in the role of permanent receivers (Goldberg, 1991). Even though skill levels should be approximately equal, there are benefits to having diversity in sex, culture, and educational backgrounds.

Patient-specific consultations. We believe that psychotherapists should adopt a low threshold for deciding to seek consultation for particularly difficult patients. Consultation

Exhibit 1

Essential Points for Consultants to Consider

The consultant should consider the following elements in his or her recommendations.
Medical/medication needs
Overall management of the case
Specific concerns/uncertainties
Therapeutic alliance and transference/countertransference issues
Crisis intervention plans in case of emergency
Alternative/additional therapeutic interventions
Risk benefit analysis of the treatment plan
Ethical/legal dimensions of the case

Copyright 1994 by Erlbaum. From *Ethics and Behavior* by Clayton and Bongar. Adapted with permission.

should be sought any time it would likely result in a noticeably improved treatment for the patient. In addition to ongoing peer consultation regarding cases, it may be desirable to have a specialist consult with a particularly difficult patient. At times, it may be desirable to have the consultant interview the patient directly. Many patients are reluctant to agree to such consultations, so it may be necessary to have a chart review or direct discussions between the provider and consultant.

Clayton and Bongar (1994) have described the ethical, legal, and clinical considerations in using consultation, and they have identified the essential points that a consultant should cover. These points, which are characterized by the acronym MOST CARE, are summarized in Exhibit 1.

The consultant should be an individual with expertise or training superior to or different from that of the provider. For example, a psychiatrist, who has superior training in the biological bases of behavior, may be able to assist with a patient being treated by a psychologist. In addition to being able to give general opinions concerning the diagnosis of the patient, a psychiatrist might be better able to assess the potential benefits of medication or to identify any medical mimics of psychological problems. Conversely, a psychiatrist may benefit from the perspective of a psychologist who, with different training and greater emphasis on psychodiagnostic testing, may be able to offer a new interpretation of the patient's problems and suggest alternative or supplementary treatments.

For the consultation to be helpful, it must be made in good faith. One of the authors [S.K.] has provided hundreds of professional consultations over the last several years. Most of the psychologists seeking the consultations do so in good faith. However, some appear to slant the information provided to justify a predetermined course of action. Additionally, the consultation should be formal and include a written report or at least a summary of the conclusions. Often friends do not make the best consultants. Although they may be comfortable to talk to and their goodwill is trusted, they may be loathe to criticize their friends.

Supervision

As defined earlier, supervision entails the authority of one practitioner to control the work product of another. Many licensing boards have standards for what constitutes the minimally acceptable degree of monitoring or control over supervised employees or trainees. These standards address the number of supervisees permitted per supervisor, the number of hours of direct supervision a week, the amount and type of documentation required, or other objective criteria. The quality of monitoring depends largely on the initiative of the supervisor.

Inadequate supervision is probably one of the most common sources of substandard treatment. The sensitive, caring, and respectful attitude of most mental health professionals has to be balanced with an understanding that their greater training and experience require them to select supervisees with due care and to assert themselves in maintaining standards of treatment.

Except under very limited circumstances, such as when the supervisee is licensed for independent practice, supervisors are responsible for the entire work product of all their supervisees. Supervisees, by the very nature of their status as defined here, have no legal authority to engage in the independent treatment of patients. They exist as treatment agents only by way of being an extension of the supervisors. Negligent behavior on the part of the supervisees could result in a charge of negligence made against the supervisor (e.g., *Montoya v. Bebensee*, 1988). The standard of care required for patients will not be lessened because a trainee is providing the care. A trainee or employee is held to the same standard of care as a licensed professional. For example, in *Emory University v. Porubiansky* (1981), the Georgia Supreme Court concluded that the status of a university as a training institution did not lower the standard of care required in treating dental patients.

Liability could be imposed if the supervisor had failed to monitor the treatment of the patient or gave inappropriate advice about the diagnosis or treatment of the patient. Liability on the basis of negligent supervision was raised in the case of *Cosgrove v. Lawrence* (1987) when a social worker had sexual intercourse with a patient on numerous occasions, including at both the mental health facility and other locations. Similarly, in *Andrews v. United States* (1982) a physician's assistant and a physician who supervised him were both found liable. The physician's assistant had developed a sexual relationship with a patient, and one of the staff physicians did not adequately investigate the complaint when he heard about it from another patient. The supervising physician probably would not have been liable if he had made reasonable efforts to investigate the allegation, such as speaking with the patient involved. Direct liability could also occur if the supervisor assigned a task to a trainee whom the supervisor knew or should have known did not have the skill to implement it properly (Harrar, VandeCreek, & Knapp, 1990).

Conscientious supervisors need to screen and monitor the patients of their supervisees with great care, at least initially, until the level of competence of the supervisees is understood. Sometimes supervisees present themselves as caring persons with adequate clinical judgment and sound interpersonal skills. However, the same supervisees may have some of the very inaccurate beliefs about child abuse and memory formation that have been reviewed in this book.

One of the authors [S.K.] received a comment from a psychologist and supervisor who met with a newly hired supervisee. The supervisee reported on a case of multiple personality disorder as a result of Satanic Ritual Abuse (SRA) as if it were common knowledge that SRA was widespread. Fortunately, this supervisor was able to identify the preconceptions on the part of the supervisee early in the treatment process. The supervisor immediately placed the burden on the supervisee to justify the diagnosis of Dissociative Identity Disorder based on *DSM-IV* (American Psychiatric Association, 1994) criteria and to justify the assumption of SRA.

Conclusion

In addition to the usual reasons to keep good records, psychotherapists can reduce their risk of malpractice judgments and ethics violations if they carefully document their care of use of memory retrieval and treatment techniques that have little or no scientific or professional basis. Documentation of informed consent is essential for protecting oneself from lawsuits. The consultation and supervisory guidelines reviewed here will help psychologists provide a high level of care to their patients. In addition to the intrinsic value of providing quality treatment to patients, the consultation and supervisory practices will provide evidence that the psychologist was attempting to adhere to high standards of treatment if his or her practices are ever called into question through a malpractice suit or charge of an ethics violation. Documentation, consultation, and supervision protect both the patient and the psychotherapist.

Chapter

7

Public Policy Considerations

Many of the criticisms leveled at the psychotherapy professions as a result of the false memory debate are exaggerated. Critics have charged that a "recovered memory industry" is manufacturing a crisis of child abuse to generate more referrals and more money for itself. They have referred to the creation of false memories as an "epidemic" and have proposed draconian remedies, such as the Mental Health Consumers Protection Act (National Association for Consumer Protection in Mental Health Practices, 1994).

Although the Mental Health Consumers Protection Act (the model act for other similar acts in various states) is a poor solution, there is a problem of substandard treatment offered to patients. A small minority of mental health practitioners treat multiple cases of repressed memory, hold unscientific notions about the process of memory, adhere to unscientific beliefs concerning a predictive cluster of symptoms, and use highly questionable techniques to recover lost memories (Polusny & Follette, 1996). Although we know of no data on this, we suspect that a small minority of licensed psychologists violate the ethical principles of their profession by perceiving themselves primarily as advocates rather than as psychotherapists.

Furthermore, a larger number of unlicensed practitioners fail to understand or apply the very basic tenets of psychotherapy and unwittingly harm patients by creating false memories of child abuse, encouraging confrontations or lawsuits against innocent parents, or otherwise disrupting the lives of their patients. Changes are needed to improve the quality of treatment provided to patients. This chapter reviews the shortcomings of the Mental Health Consumers Protection Act and then focuses on more credible responses that can improve the quality of treatment provided to patients.

Shortcomings of the Mental Health Consumers Protection Act

Since 1993, at least four state legislatures (Colorado, Illinois, New Hampshire, and Missouri) have seen the introduction of mental health consumers protection bills. These bills would require extensive informed consent procedures, deny third party reimbursement for procedures that are not scientifically validated, permit lawsuits by third parties such as parents of patients, ban pseudo-science from the courtroom, and criminalize the willful or reckless induction of false memories of abuse.

Requiring Informed Consent

One provision would mandate all psychotherapists to obtain the informed consent of their patients before starting psychotherapy. Although we have argued that informed consent (or patient participation in treatment decisions) is an essential facet of ethical behavior, this bill defines informed consent in an unnecessarily complex and countertherapeutic manner. It requires giving the patient a list of alternative treatments; a summary of the foreseeable risks, hazards, and benefits of the treatment; a signed treatment plan; and specific journal citations demonstrating that the proposed treatment has been proven reasonably safe and effective by reliable and valid scientific research studies. These studies would include treatment outcome research comparing the proposed treatment with alternative treatments and control subjects receiving no treatment (State of New Hampshire, House Bill 236, 1995).

The exhaustive disclosure of treatment alternatives and journal citations is impractical. The patient would be unlikely to absorb all the details, and the explanation would reduce the time available for patient care. Furthermore, the bill does not allow for delaying the disclosure during times of crisis and allows no flexibility regarding what is given to the patients depending on their individual needs. Nor does the bill allow for changes in the treatment plan depending on changes in the life circumstances of the patient or the revelation of additional problems. Finally, it fails to recognize that many patients may not have had the highly circumscribed diagnoses found in controlled outcome studies.

The informed consent standards found in the ethics code of the American Psychological Association (1992) are much more reasonable. These standards require that

> when psychologists provide assessment, evaluation, treatment, counseling, supervision, teaching, consultation, research, or other psychological services to an individual, a group, or an organization, they provide, using language that is reasonably understandable to the recipient of these services, appropriate information beforehand about the nature of such services and appropriate information later about results and conclusions. (Standard 1.07a)

Standard 4.02 provides further guidance for psychologists:

> (a) Psychologists obtain appropriate informed consent to therapy or related procedures, using language that is reasonably understandable to participants. The content of informed consent will vary depending on many circumstances; however, informed consent generally implies that the person (1) has the capacity to consent, (2) has been informed of significant information concerning the procedure, (3) has freely and without undue influence expressed consent, and (4) consent has been appropriately documented. (APA, 1992)

Requiring Scientifically Based Treatments

The Mental Health Consumers Protection Act would prohibit insurance reimbursement for therapy based on principles that are not scientifically validated. This provision ignores the sophistication required for the practice of psychotherapy. Although mental health professionals base their treatments on scientifically proven principles as much as possible, science has not yet validated particular treatments for all patients for all disorders (or all combinations of disorders).

Even when scientific evidence supports the overall efficacy of one or more treatments, the literature shows that some patients do not respond adequately to the suggested treatment. Secondary or tertiary diagnoses, life circumstances, intelligence levels, and other patient characteristics may suggest the need to modify the original treatment. For example, it may be fruitful for a psychotherapist to involve a spouse or significant other, a parent, or a grandparent in the cognitive treatment of depression for a young adult. Although this option may not be specified by a standard treatment protocol, it would be done in a manner consistent with cognitive theory. However, it is unclear how much deviation from the protocol would be permitted before the "official treatment" would be considered to no longer be in use.

Psychotherapy is not a technical skill that only requires the application of a few algorithms or cookbook solutions to the problems of patients. It is seldom possible to ascertain a diagnosis or design a treatment plan for a patient on the basis of rigid forced-choice questions. Instead, formulating the diagnosis and treatment plan requires expertise and judgment, depending on the unique attributes or characteristics of each patient. Again, the American Psychological Association's (1992) ethics code presents a much more appropriate standard: "Psychotherapists rely on scientifically and professionally derived knowledge when making scientific or professional judgments ..." (Standard 1.06).

Advocates of the Mental Health Consumers Protection Act claim they are only trying to hold psychotherapists to the same scientific standards as medical doctors. However, the conclusions based on that analogy are inappropriate. Other than a few common ailments, the practice of medicine also requires considerable judgment on the part of the physician. Furthermore, there are controversies about the efficacy of many medical procedures (prostatectomies, mammograms, etc.) or the application of specific medications such as antidepressants to the treatment of nondepressive disorders (Ciocca, 1995).

Finally, the advancement of psychology as a science requires the controlled application and measurement of new methods of treatment. The prohibition against unproven techniques would prevent any advancement of psychology as a science. Once again, the ethics code of the American Psychological Association (1992) provides a more reasoned standard:

> In those emerging areas in which generally recognized standards for preparatory training do not yet exist, psychologists nevertheless take reasonable steps to ensure the competence of their work and to protect patients ... and others from harm. (Standard 1.04)

Allowing Third-Party Lawsuits

These bills would permit lawsuits by third parties who perceive themselves to be injured by psychotherapy (or by the patient who is undergoing psychotherapy). Currently, the only generally recognized basis for third-party suits is the "duty to protect" rule (*Tarasoff* doctrine; *Tarasoff v. The Regents of the University of California et al.*, 1976), wherein psychotherapists have to act to protect "identifiable third parties" from the imminent danger of substantial physical harm. The *Tarasoff* doctrine has not been applied to instances of threatened emotional harm created by interpersonal strife.

The third-party suit provision would inhibit the success of psychotherapy without providing a comparable social benefit. The lives of patients, as do the lives of all persons, include interpersonal strife. Parents get angry at their children and vice versa; spouses get angry at each other and sometimes get divorced; and employers and employees do not always get along. The third-party suit provision would allow any person in conflict with patients to "get even" by alleging harm. An aggrieved third party could initiate a suit at any time and compromise the confidentiality and effectiveness of psychotherapy. For example, a wife who suspects that her husband is planning to leave her (or a husband who is dissatisfied with the way his wife treats him), could initiate a lawsuit and force the disclosure of the content of psychotherapy.

Banning Pseudo-Science from the Courtroom

The model act would also ban pseudo-science from the courtroom. This provision states that no therapy procedure or therapeutic information should be permitted as expert testimony unless a substantial majority of the scientific community (not the psychotherapy or practitioner community) validates it. It is not clear which scientific community is being referenced (Hinnefeld, 1996). Would a psychotherapy research project be considered part of the psychotherapy or scientific community? Furthermore, the bill would place limits on what judges can or cannot accept as expert testimony to help them decide cases. It is more prudent to let courts rely on existing rules of evidence to determine which experts to admit. Opposing attorneys are quite capable of challenging the appropriateness of any testimony introduced in court.

Criminalizing the Reckless Induction of False Memories

Finally, the model act would criminalize the reckless induction of false accusations of abuse. The terms "reckless" and "false" are not defined, and it is impossible to know ahead of time what they constitute. Is it a false memory when an adult recalls being victimized by being forced to engage in both oral and vaginal sex, when the corroborating evidence can only prove that she was forced to engage in vaginal sex? The "reckless" implanting of memories should be determined in specific malpractice cases in which expert witnesses testify after having looked at the context of the techniques used. Because the malpractice insurance policies of mental health practitioners typically do not cover criminal acts, threats of criminal charges for recklessly inducing memories would intimidate providers because even an accusation of implanting abuse could result in costly legal fees (Hinnefeld, 1996). Furthermore, adults who recovered memories of childhood abuse and talked about their experiences outside of the psychotherapy room would run the risk of having their psychotherapists sued for "recklessly inducing" these memories.

More Adequate Controls
Over Psychotherapy

Our opposition to the Mental Health Consumers Protection Act should not be interpreted to mean that we believe that all is well with the practice of psychotherapy. We oppose the Mental Health Consumers Protection Act because it would limit the effectiveness of psychotherapy without providing for comparable social benefits. Other changes would be more effective in improving the quality of treatment available to consumers.

Changes are needed in the mechanisms by which psychotherapy is regulated. The mechanisms by which professions are governed include before-the-fact controls (e.g., educational standards, licensing examinations, mandatory continuing education), which prevent harmful acts against patients, and after-the-fact controls (ethics committees, malpractice cases, disciplinary actions before the state licensing boards), which remediate or punish professionals after misconduct has occurred.

It is always preferable to use before-the-fact controls so that no patients are harmed at all. We call for greater before-the-fact control over unlicensed psychotherapists. Second, we call for better enforcement of existing before-the-fact controls over the professionals who are already licensed.

Greater Control Over Unlicensed Professionals

Lower levels of training appear to lead to poorer quality of treatment for patients. Anecdotal reports suggest that the extreme cases of negligent memory work come from untrained and unlicensed professionals (Lindsay & Read, 1995). For example, the psychotherapist who helped Stephen Cook recover memories of abuse by Cardinal Bernadin received a master's degree from an unaccredited university ("Bernardin Case," 1994). Fortunately, Mr. Cook learned that the methods used to help him recover those memories were faulty, and he dropped the suit against the Cardinal. In addition, available survey data are consistent with the notion that undertrained individuals provide an overall lower quality of care. For example, the 1995 *Consumer Reports* study (Seligman, 1995) of psychotherapy found that the outcome for marriage and family therapists was poorer than it was for the psychologists, psychiatrists, and social workers.

Some may argue that marriage and family counselors have a harder job because they deal with divorce and troubled marriages, which inherently make a positive outcome more difficult. However, the same *Consumer Reports* study found that patients sought treatments from marriage and family therapists for generally the same types of problems for which they sought treatment from the other mental health professionals (Seligman, 1995). Although some might argue that there is a need to change the education or licensing standards for marriage and family therapists, this issue is only one aspect of a larger problem of unqualified psychotherapists. As shown in Table 4, there are grounds for believing that some psychologists, social workers, and, to a lesser extent, psychiatrists are involved in creating false memories ("Research Notes," 1993). Nonetheless, a disproportionate number of false memory claims appear to come from patients treated by miscellaneous unlicensed psychotherapists and counselors.

Data from McMinn and Wade (1995) also support the idea that undertrained psychotherapists are responsible for a disproportionate number of allegations of false memories.

Table 4

Professional Affiliations of Psychotherapists Alleged To Have Implanted False Memories

Affiliation	*Total Respondents To Survey	**Total Alleged To Have Created False Memories of Abuse
Psychologists	37%	25%
Psychiatrists	22%	9%
Social Workers	14%	18%
Marriage & Family Therapists	9%	—
Other Counselors	18%	48%

Note. *Data from Seligman, M. (1995). The Effectiveness of Psychotherapy: The *Consumer Reports* Study. *American Psychologist, 50,* 965–974.
**Data from "Research Notes." (1993). *False Memory Foundation Newsletter, 2,* 10–11.

McMinn and Wade (1995) found that 2.4% of the patients seen by unlicensed psychotherapists were believed to have been survivors of satanic ritual abuse (SRA) compared with .05% of a sample of psychologists from the APA's Division 17 (Counseling Psychology).

Greater controls need to be placed on unqualified professionals. Most state licensing laws have exemptions that allow unlicensed and untrained psychotherapists or counselors to practice without regulation. Their training varies considerably from master's degrees (or perhaps doctoral degrees from unaccredited universities) to bachelor's degrees or less. They have no licensing examination to pass, no supervised work experience, and no well-defined body of knowledge to acquire before they begin to provide public service. Therefore we first recommend to bar the practice of psychotherapy or counseling by any person who is not licensed, is not working under the direct supervision of a licensed professional, or is not working in an agency that is exempted from licensure because it includes adequate safeguards to ensure the quality of patient care.

Greater Controls Over Licensed Professionals

Although unqualified psychotherapists are responsible for a disproportionate amount of negligent treatment, an unacceptable amount of negligent treatment also occurs among licensed professionals. Professionals who are already licensed need to improve the mechanisms by which the quality of treatment is monitored. It is necessary for training programs to ensure an adequate understanding of the ethical principles of the profession and to ensure that their curricula include a strong adherence to scientific reasoning, to the scientific bases of behavior, and to disciplined inquiry.

Therefore we recommend that professional training programs re-emphasize their commitment to the scientific method and to disciplined inquiry as means of continuing to improve the quality of the treatments provided to patients. Ethical violations are not always committed by uncaring or unsympathetic providers. In fact, the proponents of unscientific techniques are often altruistic and well-meaning people who have a great deal of empathy and concern for their patients. Major problems occur, however, when they fail to understand their proper role as psychotherapists and engage in boundary violations by becoming more advocate than therapist.

Finally we recommend that licensing boards require proof of a separate course on professional ethics for every first-time applicant for the licensing examination. In addition, we recommend that licensure boards require evidence of continuing education in ethics whenever their ethics codes are modified in substantive ways.

Conclusion

Although there may be shortcomings in the training of some psychologists, the present educational and licensing institutions have the ability to redress these shortcomings. The need for regulation of unlicensed counselors and psychotherapists is more pressing. However, the proposed Mental Health Consumers Protection Act is not a viable option to protect consumers. Instead, it would impede the ability of patients to access quality treatment.

Chapter

8

Conclusion

Unfortunately, the controversy over repressed or false memories has been characterized by harsh rhetoric and outlandish claims on both sides of the debate. The antitherapy rhetoric in the "repressed memory war" has often been unjustified and needlessly offensive. The attack on psychotherapy may have had a chilling effect on competent and conscientious professionals who want to provide legitimate services to survivors of childhood abuse. Furthermore, some supporters have endorsed legislation that would place draconian standards on psychotherapy and vitiate its effectiveness.

However, some of the false memory controversy is due to the use of misguided techniques on the part of some psychotherapists. The procedures of some psychotherapists are inconsistent with basic scientific information about memory formation and retrieval and contradict acceptable professional standards of conduct. These substandard practices lack empirical or professional support for their effectiveness and have led in some cases to false accusations of abuse against the family members of patients.

In writing this book, we have tried to look beyond the polarity found in the current "false" versus "repressed" memory debate, and have focused on three main points. First, we believe that psychotherapists who work in accordance with acceptable professional standards have minimal risks of being charged with ethics complaints or negligent practice. Second, we argue that good psychotherapy needs to be practiced in accordance with the scientific understanding of human behavior. Finally, we have advocated for effective controls over psychotherapy designed to ensure public access to quality psychotherapy services.

Competent Psychotherapy Is Safe Psychotherapy

Some psychotherapists who treat adult survivors of childhood abuse may perceive themselves as being caught between a rock and a hard place. Although they feel committed to providing quality services, they may perceive that they place themselves in legal jeopardy when treating this patient population. We have tried to correct this misconception.

Our legal review shows that competent psychotherapists should not be intimidated into refraining from treating adult survivors of childhood abuse. Professionals who adhere to appropriate professional boundaries and who rely on scientific and professionally acceptable methods of diagnosing and treating patients provide quality treatment to their patients with minimal legal risks to themselves.

Psychotherapy Should Be Based on Behavioral Science

We have also emphasized the importance of understanding basic information about memory formation and retrieval. There is much that is known about the development of memory for ordinary experiences; however, "there are gaps in our knowledge about the processes that lead to accurate and inaccurate recollections of childhood sexual abuse" (Alpert et al., 1996, p. 1). The quality of treatment given to patients and their families will improve as the size of the knowledge gap is reduced.

Professional psychotherapists need researchers to help elucidate the psychological processes involved in memory formation and retrieval. Professional psychology should be scientifically informed. Researchers need professional psychotherapists to identify the important issues faced by their patients, to challenge the relevance of their research, and to provide the clinical lore that either supports or contradicts the theories they develop. The questions addressed by researchers should be practice informed.

Greater Public Protections Are Needed

Although we reject the Mental Health Consumers Protection Act (National Association for Consumer Protection in Mental Health Practices, 1994) as a legitimate means to protect public interests, we believe that changes are needed to ensure minimal standards of treatment for all patients. Controls should be placed over unlicensed professionals who are practicing without a government licensing board to establish minimum entry credentials, require continuing education, and discipline unethical or incompetent practitioners. In addition, greater controls should be placed over currently licensed professionals to ensure that they have acquired basic information about the scientific underpinnings of behavior, understand controlled psychotherapy outcome research, and adhere to the ethical standards of their professions.

References

Accusations. (1993, May). *FMS Foundation Newsletter, 2,* p. 9.

Alabama Supreme Court rejects *McDuffie* appeal in malpractice case regarding third party standing. (1995, November/December). *FMS Foundation Newsletter, 4,* 9.

Alpert, J. (1996). Professional practice, psychological science, and the delayed memory debate. In J. Alpert (Ed.), *Sexual abuse recalled: Treating trauma in the era of the recovered memory debate* (pp. 3–28). Northvale, NJ: Aronson.

Alpert, J., Brown, L., & Courtois, C. (1996). Symptomatic clients and memories of childhood abuse: What the trauma and child sexual abuse literature tells us. In J. L. Alpert, L. S. Brown, S. J. Ceci, C. A. Courtois, E. F. Loftus, & P. A. Ornstein (Eds.), *American Psychological Association working group on investigation of memories of childhood abuse* (pp. 15–105). Washington, DC: American Psychological Association.

Alpert, J. L., Brown, L. S., Ceci, S. J., Courtois, C. A., Loftus, E. F., & Ornstein, P. A. (Eds.). (1996). *Working group on investigation of memories of childhood abuse: Final report.* Washington, DC: Author.

American Psychiatric Association. (1986). *Principles of medical ethics with annotations especially applicable to psychiatry.* Washington, DC: Author.

American Psychiatric Association. (1993, December 12). *Statement on memories of sexual abuse.* Washington, DC: Author.

American Psychiatric Association. (1994). *Diagnostic and statistical manual* (4th ed.). Washington, DC: Author.

American Psychological Association. (1992). Ethical principles of psychologists and code of conduct. *American Psychologist, 47,* 1597–1611.

Andrews v. United States, 548 F. Supp. 603 (1982).

Australian Psychological Society. (1994, October 1). *Guidelines relating to recovered memories.* Sydney, Australia: Author.

Barden, C. (1994, December 1). *Supporters of the National Association for Consumer Protection in Mental Health Practices.* Unpublished letter and memo.

Barden, C. (1994, December 7). *Letter to the Honorable William Goodling, Committee for Labor and Education, United States Congress.* Unpublished letter.

Bass, E., & Davis, L. (1988). *The courage to heal.* New York: Harper & Row.

Bass, E., & Davis, L. (1994). *The courage to heal* (3rd ed.). New York: Harper & Row.

Becker, J., Alpert, J., BigFoot, D. S., Bonner, B., Geddie, L., Henggler, S., Kaufman, K., & Walker, C. E. (1995). Empirical research on child abuse treatment: Report by the Child Abuse and Neglect Treatment Working

Group, American Psychological Association. *Journal of Clinical Child Psychology, 24*(Suppl.), 23–46.

Berger, K. S., & Thompson, R. (1995). *The developing person through childhood and adolescence.* New York: Worth.

Berliner, L., & Loftus, E. (1992). Sexual abuse accusations: Desperately seeking reconciliation. *Journal of Interpersonal Violence, 7,* 570–578.

Bernardin Case. (1994, February). *FMS Foundation Newsletter, 3,* 12.

Beutler, L., Williams, R., & Zetzer, H. (1994). Efficacy of treatment for victims of child sexual abuse. *The Future of Children, 4,* 157–174.

Bird v. W.C.W., 868 S.W.2d 767 (Tex. 1994).

Bloom, P. (1994). Clinical guidelines in using hypnosis in uncovering memories of sexual abuse: A master class commentary. *International Journal of Clinical and Experimental Hypnosis, 62,* 173–178.

Briere, J. (1992). *Child abuse trauma.* Thousand Oaks, CA: Sage.

Briere, J., & Conte, J. (1993). Self-reported amnesia for abuse in adults molested as children. *Journal of Traumatic Stress, 6,* 21–31.

British Psychological Society. (1995). *Recovered memories: The report of the working party of the British Psychological Society.* Leicester, England: Author.

Brown, D. (1994). Pseudomemories: The standard of science and the standard of care in trauma treatment. *American Journal of Clinical Psychology, 37,* 1–24.

Butler, K. (1995, March/April). Caught in the cross fire. *The Family Networker, 19*(2), 24–34, 68–79.

Byrd, I. (1994). The narrative construction of child abuse survivors. *American Psychologist, 49,* 439–440.

Canterbury v. Spence, 464 F. Supp. 772 (D.C. Cir. 1972).

Caudill, O. B. (1994, August). Response for defendant in *Roberts v. Los Altos Hospital.* Superior Court, Los Angeles, South District, Case No. NC014592.

Caudill, O. B. (1995, February). *The repressed memory war.* Presentation made at the Annual Meeting of the California Psychological Association, LaJolla, CA.

Ciocca, M. (1995, March). President's message: New threats to your practice. *Newsletter of the New Hampshire Psychological Organization, 8*(2), 6–7.

Clayton, S., & Bongar, B. (1994). The use of consultation in psychological practice: Ethical, legal, and clinical considerations. *Ethics and Behavior, 4,* 43–57.

Clevenger, N. (1991–1992). Statute of limitations: Childhood victims of sexual abuse bringing civil actions against their perpetrators after attaining the age of majority. *Journal of Family Law, 30,* 447–469.

Clute, S. (1993). Adult survivor litigation as an integral part of the therapeutic process. *Journal of Child Sexual Abuse, 2,* 121–127.

Cobb v. Grant, 502 P.2d 1 (1972).

Coons, P. (1994). Reports of satanic ritual abuse: Further implications about pseudomemories. *Perceptual and Motor Skills, 78,* 1376–1378.

Cosgrove v. Lawrence, 522 A.2d 483 (N.J. Super. A.D. 1987).

Couple Brings Suit Over Malpractice in New Hampshire. (1995, June). *FMS Foundation Newsletter, 4,* 12–13.

Cruz-Lat, E. (1994a, April 7). Witness: Therapist misrepresented herself as eating disorder specialist. *The Napa Valley Register,* p. 1.

Cruz-Lat, E. (1994b, April 30). Truth serum? *The Napa Valley Register,* p. 1A.

Davis, L. (1990). *The courage to heal workbook.* New York: Harper & Row.

Donaldson, M. A., & Cordes-Green, S. (1994). *Group treatment of adult incest survivors.* Thousand Oaks, CA: Sage.

Elliott, D. M., & Briere, J. (1995). Posttraumatic stress associated with delayed recall of sexual abuse: A general population study. *Journal of Traumatic Stress, 8,* 629–647.

Emory University v. Porubiansky, 282 S.E.2d 903 (Ga. 1981).

Faigman, D. (1995). The evidentiary status of social science under *Daubert:* Is it "scientific," "technical," or "other knowledge?" *Psychology, Public Policy, and Law, 1,* 960–979.

False Memory Syndrome Foundation and Johns Hopkins Medical Center. (1995). Basic standards of care in diagnostic and therapeutic practices with memory and the process of family reconciliation [Conference Brochure] (p. 2). San Diego, CA: Author.

Family Survey Update. (1994, June). *FMS Foundation Newsletter, 3,* 17.

Feldman-Summers, S., & Pope, K. (1994). The experience of "forgetting" childhood abuse: A national survey of psychologists. *Journal of Consulting and Clinical Psychology, 62,* 636–639.

Finkelhor, D., & Dzubia-Leatherman, J. (1994). Victimization of children. *American Psychologist, 49,* 173–183.

Fox, R. (1995). The rape of psychology. *Professional Psychology: Research and Practice, 27,* 147–155.

Fredrickson, R. (1992). *Repressed memories: A journey to recovery from sexual abuse.* New York: Fireside/Parkside.

Freeland, A., Manchanda, R., Chiu, S., Sharma, V., & Merskey, H. (1993). Four cases of supposed multiple personality disorder: Evidence of unjustified diagnoses. *Canadian Journal of Psychiatry, 38,* 245–247.

Freyd, J. (1994). Betrayal trauma: Traumatic amnesia as an adaptive response to childhood abuse. *Ethics and Behavior, 4,* 307–329.

Freyd, P. (In press). The False Memory Syndrome Foundation: Response to a mental health crisis. In D. A. Halperin (Ed.), *False memory syndrome: Therapeutic and forensic perspectives.* Washington, DC: American Psychiatric Press.

Galanter, M. (1988). Zealous self-help groups as adjuncts to psychiatric treatment: A study of Recovery, Inc. *American Journal of Psychiatry, 145,* 1248–1253.

Girl recants tales of abuse; therapist, confidants sued. (1994, December 14). *Harrisburg Patriot News*, p. B5.

Gold, S. N., Hughes, D., & Hohnecker, L. (1994). Degrees of repression of sexual abuse memories. *American Psychologist, 49*, 441–442.

Goldberg, C. (1991). *On becoming a psychotherapist*. Northvale, NJ: Aronson.

Goldstein, E., & Farmer, K. (Eds.). (1993). *True stories of false memories*. Boca Raton, FL: Social Issues Resources Service.

Goldstein, E., & Farmer, K. (Eds.). (1994). *Confabulations: Creating false memories; destroying families*. Boca Raton, FL: Social Issues Resources Service.

Grinker, R., & Spiegel, J. (1945). *War neurosis*. Philadelphia: Blakiston.

Guthiel, T. (1993). True or false memories of sexual abuse? A forensic psychiatric view. *Psychiatric Annals, 9*, 527–531.

Guthiel, T. (1995). Risk management and recovered memories. *Psychiatric Services, 46*(6), 537.

Hamanne v. Humenansky. Second Judicial District, Minnesota, C4-94-203 (1995).

Hammond, D. C. (1995). Hypnosis, false memories and guidelines for using hypnosis with potential victims of abuse. In J. Alpert (Ed.), *Sexual abuse recalled: Treating trauma in the era of the recovered memory debate* (pp. 101–131). Northvale, NJ: Aronson.

Hammond, D. C., Garver, R. B., Mutter, C. B., Crasilneck, H. B., Frischolz, E., Gravitz, M. A., Hibler, N. S., Olson, J., Scheflin, A., Spiegel, H., & Wester, W. (1994). *Clinical hypnosis and memory: Guidelines for clinicians and for forensic hypnosis*. Washington, DC: American Society of Clinical Hypnosis Press.

Harrar, W., VandeCreek, L., & Knapp, S. (1990). Ethical and legal aspects of clinical supervision. *Professional Psychology: Research and Practice, 21*, 37–41.

Harvey, M R., & Herman, J. L. (1994). Amnesia, partial amnesia, and delayed recall among adult survivors of childhood trauma. *Counsciousness and Cognition, 3*, 295–306.

Helling v. Carey, 519 P.2d 981 (1974).

Herman, J. (1992). *Trauma and recovery*. New York: Basic Books.

Herman, J., & Schatzow, E. (1987). Recovery and verification of memories of childhood sexual trauma. *Psychoanalytic Psychology, 4*, 1–14.

Hinnefeld, B. (1996, January 22). *Mental Health Consumers Protection Act* [Unpublished memo], Practice Directorate, American Psychological Association, Washington, DC.

Hintzman, D. (1978). *The psychology of learning and memory*. New York: Freeman.

Hyman, I., Husband, R., & Billings, F. J. (1995). False memories of childhood experiences. *Applied Cognitive Psychology, 9*, 181–197.

Jablonski v. United States, 12 F. 391 (9th Cir. 1983).

Johnson, M., Hashtroudi, S., & Lindsay, S. (1993). Source monitoring. *Psychological Bulletin, 114*, 3–28.

Johnson v. Johnson, 701 F. Supp. 1363 (N.D. Ill. 1988).

Joyce-Couch v. DeSilva, 602 N.E.2d 286 (Ohio App. 1991).

Keenan, M. (1995, June 22–28). The Devil & Dr. Braun. *New City*, pp. 9–11.

Khatian v. Jones, (1994). Dallas County Texas, 9th Judicial District, No. 90-14035-D.

Kluft, R. P. (1996). Treating the traumatic memories of patients with dissociative identity disorder. *American Journal of Psychiatry, 153*, 103–110.

Knapp, S. (1994). *Summary of the complaints before the Ethics Committee of the Pennsylvania Psychological Association.* Unpublished manuscript.

Knapp, S., & VandeCreek, L. (1994). *Anxiety disorders: A scientific approach for selecting the most effective treatment.* Sarasota, FL: Professional Resource Press.

Lanning, K. (1992). A law enforcement perspective on allegations of ritual abuse. In D. Sakheim & S. Devine (Eds.), *Out of darkness: Exploring Satanism and ritual abuse* (pp. 109–146). New York: Lexington.

Latz, T., Kramer, S., & Hughes, D. (1995). Multiple personality disorder among female inpatients in a state hospital. *American Journal of Psychiatry, 152*, 1343–1348.

Laurence, J. R., & Perry, C. (1983). Hypnotically created memory among highly hypnotizable subjects. *Science, 222*, 523–524.

Legal Actions Against Parents. (1994, February). *FMS Foundation Newsletter, 3*, 9.

Lief, H., & Fetkewicz, J. (1995). Retractors of false memories: The evolution of pseudo-memories. *Psychiatry and the Law, 23*, 411–436.

Lindsay, D. S., & Read, D. (1995). "Memory work" and recovered memories of childhood sexual abuse: Scientific evidence and public, professional, and personal issues. *Psychology, Public Policy and Law, 1*, 846–908.

Lipinski, J. F., & Pope, H. G. (1994). Do flashbacks represent obsessional imagery? *Comprehensive Psychiatry, 35*(4), 245–247.

Loftus, E. (1993). The reality of repressed memories. *American Psychologist, 48*, 518–537.

Loftus, E. (1994). The repressed memory controversy. *American Psychologist, 49*, 443–445.

Loftus, E. (1995). Remembering dangerously. *Skeptical Inquirer, 19*(2), 20–29.

Loftus, E., Polonksy, S., & Fullilove, M. (1994). Memories of childhood sexual abuse: Remembering and repressing. *Psychology of Women Quarterly, 18*, 67–84.

Loftus, E., & Ketcham, K. (1994). *The myth of repressed memories.* New York: St. Martin's Press.

London, R. (1995). Therapeutic treatment of repressed memories. *The Independent Practitioner, 15*(2), 64–67.

Malpractice lawsuit against therapist settles. (1995, November/December). *FMS Foundation Newsletter, 4*, 11.

Maltsberger, J. (1993). A career plundered. *Suicide and Life-Threatening Behavior, 23*, 285–291.

Maltz, W. (1992). *The sexual healing journey: A guide for survivors of sexual abuse.* New York: Harper Collins.

Marine, E., & Caudill, O. B. (1994). *What really happened?* Amityville, NY: American Professional Agency.

Martinez-Taboas, A. (1996). Repressed memories: Some clinical data contributing toward its elucidation. *American Journal of Psychotherapy, 50*, 217–230.

Mayer, R. (1995). Treating the very difficult sexual abuse survivor. In M. Hunter (Ed.), *Adult survivors of sexual abuse: Treatment innovations* (pp. 83–97). Newbury Park, CA: Sage.

McElroy, S., & Keck, P. (1995). Misattribution of eating and obsessive-compulsive disorder symptoms to repressed memories of childhood sexual or physical abuse. *Biological Psychiatry, 37*, 48–51.

McHugh, P. (1993, September). Multiple personality disorder. *The Harvard Mental Health Letter, 10*(3), 1.

McMillen, C., Zuravin, S., & Rideout, G. (1995). Perceived benefit from child sexual abuse. *Journal of Consulting and Clinical Psychology, 63*, 1037–1043.

McMinn, M., & Wade, N. (1995). Beliefs about the prevalence of dissociative identity disorder, sexual abuse, and ritual abuse among religious and non-religious therapists. *Professional Psychology: Research and Practice, 26*, 257–261.

McNamara, E. (1994). *Breakdown: Sex, suicide, and the Harvard psychiatrist.* New York: Pocket.

McNulty, C., & Wardle, J. (1994). Adult disclosure of sexual abuse: A primary cause of psychological distress. *Child Abuse and Neglect, 18*, 549–555.

Montoya v. Bebensee, 761 P.2d 285 (Colo. App. 1988).

My Sister's Story. (1993, February). *FMS Foundation Newsletter, 2*, 8.

Nagy, T. (1994, July/August). Repressed memories: Guidelines and direction. *The National Psychologist*, p. 8.

Nash, M. (1987). What, if anything, is regressed about hypnotic age regression? A review of the empirical literature. *Psychological Bulletin, 102*, 42–52.

National Association for Consumer Protection in Mental Health Practices. (1994). *A proposal to finance preparation of model legislation titled "Mental health consumer protection act."* Unpublished manuscript.

Neisser, U., & Harsch, N. (1993). Phantom flashbulbs: False recollections of hearing the news about the Challenger. In E. Winograd & Y. Neisser (Eds.), *Affect and accuracy in recall* (pp. 9–31). New York: Cambridge University Press.

Nelson, E., & Simpson, P. (1994). First glimpse: An initial examination of subjects who have rejected their recovered visualizations as false memories. *Issues in Child Abuse Accusations, 6*, 123–133.

O'Connell, D. N., Shor, R. E., & Orne, M. T. (1970). Hypnotic age regression: An empirical and methodological analysis. *Journal of Abnormal Psychology, 76*, 1–31.

Oksana, C. (1994). *Safe passage to healing: A guide for survivors of ritual abuse.* New York: Harper-Collins.

Ornstein, P. A., Ceci, S. J., & Loftus, E. F. (1996). Adult recollections of childhood abuse: Cognitive and developmental perspectives. In J. L. Alpert, L. S. Brown, S. J. Ceci, C. A. Courtois, E. F. Loftus, & P. A. Ornstein (Eds.), *Working group on investigation of memories of childhood abuse* (pp. 150–197). Washington, DC: American Psychological Association.

Osheroff v. Chestnut Lodge, 490 A. 2d 720 (Md. App. 1985).

Overstreet, S. (1993, February). Don't conjure up traces of incest. *FMS Foundation Newsletter, 2*, 6.

Parker, J. (1993). *At the heart of darkness: Witchcraft, black magic and Satanism today.* New York: Citadel.

Paddison, P., Einbinder, R. G., Maker, E., & Strain, J. J. (1993). Group treatment with incest survivors. In P. L. Paddison (Ed.), *Treatment of adult survivors of incest* (pp. 35–52). Washington, DC: American Psychiatric Press.

Parents, Siblings Join Retractor in Lawsuit. (1996, July/August). *FMS Foundation Newsletter, 5*, 3.

Parents Tell Us. (1993, March). *FMS Foundation Newsletter, 2*, 9.

Pendergast, M. (1995). *Victims of memory: Incest accusations and shattered lives.* Hinesburg, VT: Upper Access, Inc.

Polusny, M., & Follette, V. (1996). Remembering childhood sexual abuse: A national survey of psychologists' clinical practices, beliefs, and personal experiences. *Professional Psychology: Research and Practice, 27*, 41–52.

Poole, D. A., Lindsay, D. S., Memon, A., & Bull, R. (1995). Psychotherapy and the recovery of memories of childhood sexual abuse: U.S. and British practitioners' opinions, practices, and experiences. *Journal of Consulting and Clinical Psychology, 63*, 426–437.

Poor, E. (1995, June). Couple brings suit over malpractice in New Hampshire. *FMS Foundation Newsletter, 4*, 12–13.

Pope, K. (1996). Memory, abuse, and science: Questioning claims about the false memory syndrome epidemic. *American Psychologist, 51*, 957–974.

Pope, K., & Brown, L. (1996). *Recovered memories of abuse: Assessment, therapy, forensics.* Washington, DC: American Psychological Association.

Pope, K., & Tabachnick, B. (1995). Recovered memories of abuse among therapy patients: A national survey. *Ethics and Behavior, 5*, 237–248.

Prosser, W. (1971). *Law of torts* (4th ed.). St. Paul, MN: West.

Pynoos, R. S., & Nader, K. (1989). Children's memory and proximity to violence. *Journal of American Academy of Child and Adolescent Psychiatry, 28*, 236–241.

Repressed Memory Claims Expected to Soar. (1995, May). *National Psychologist, 4*(3), 3.

Research Notes. (1993, January). *FMS Foundation Newsletter, 2*, 10–11.

Reviere, S. L. (1996). *Memory of childhood trauma: A clinician's guide to the literature.* New York, NY: Guilford.

Rogers, M. (1994). Factors to consider in assessing adult litigants' complaints of childhood sexual abuse. *Behavioural Science and the Law, 12,* 279–298.

Romans, S., Martin, J., Anderson, J., Herbison, G. P., & Mullen, P. (1995). Sexual abuse in childhood and deliberate self-harm. *American Journal of Psychiatry, 152,* 1336–1342.

Rosen, G. (1995). The Aleutian Enterprise sinking and post-traumatic stress disorder: Misdiagnosis in clinical and forensic settings. *Professional Psychology: Research and Practice, 26,* 82–87.

Ross, A. (1994, June). Blame it on the Devil. *Redbook, 183,* 86–89, 110, 114, 116.

Rubin, L. (1996). Childhood sexual abuse: False accusations of "false memory." *Professional Psychology: Research and Practice, 27,* 447–451.

Salter, A. (1995). *Transforming trauma.* Newbury Park, CA: Sage.

Schacter, D. (1995, April). Memory wars [Review of the books *Making monsters: The myth of repressed memories;* and *Victims of memory*]. *Scientific American, 274,* 135–139.

Scheflin, A., & Shapiro, J. (1989). *Trance on trial.* New York: Guilford.

Schneider, J. (1994, August). Legal issues involving "repressed memory" of childhood sexual abuse. *The Psychologists Legal Update, 5,* Washington, DC: National Register of Health Service Providers in Psychology.

Schwarz, R. (1996). Separating fact from fiction in the "false memory" question. In L. VandeCreek, S. Knapp, & T. Jackson (Eds.), *Innovations in clinical practice: A source book* (Vol. 15, pp. 13–30). Sarasota, FL: Professional Resource Press.

Seligman, M. (1995). The effectiveness of psychotherapy: The *Consumer Reports* study. *American Psychologist, 50,* 965–974.

Sheiman, J. A. (1993). "I've always wondered if something happened to me": Assessment of child sexual abuse. *Journal of Child Sexual Abuse, 2,* 13–21.

Silk, K., Lee, S., Hill, E., & Lohr, N. (1995). Borderline personality disorder symptoms and severity of sexual abuse. *American Journal of Psychiatry, 152,* 1059–1064.

Simon, R. (1992). *Clinical psychiatry and the law.* Washington, DC: American Psychiatric Association Press.

Soisson, E. L., VandeCreek, L., & Knapp, S. (1987). Thorough record keeping: A good defense in a litigious era. *Professional Psychology: Research and Practice, 18,* 498–502.

Spanos, N., Burgess, C., & Burgess, M. F. (1994). Past-life identities, UFO abductions, and satanic ritual abuse: The social construction of memories. *The International Journal of Clinical and Experimental Hypnosis, 43,* 433–446.

Spanos, N., Menary, E., Gabora, N., DuBreuil, S., & Dewhirst, B. (1991). Secondary identity enactments during hypnotic past-life regressions: A sociocognitive perspective. *Journal of Personality and Social Psychology, 61,* 308–320.

State of New Hampshire. House Bill 236 (1995).

State of New Hampshire v. Hungerford; State of New Hampshire v. Morahan. Superior court, Hillsborough County, 94-S-045 thru 94-S-047; 93-S-1734 thru 93-S-1936 (1995, May 23).

Strassburger, L., Jorgenson, P., & Sutherland, P. (1992). The prevention of psychotherapist sexual misconduct: Avoiding the slippery slope. *American Journal of Psychotherapy, 46,* 544–555.

Suits against abusive therapists settled. (1995, June). *FMS Foundation Newsletter, 4,* 11–12.

Sullivan v. Cheshier, 846 F. Supp. 654 (N.D. Ill. 1994).

Tarasoff v. The Regents of the University of California et al., 551 P.2d 334 (1976).

Terr, L. (1994). *Unchained memories.* New York: Basic.

Tuman v. Genesis, 894 F. Supp. 183 (E.D. Pa. 1995).

VandeCreek, L., & Knapp, S. (1993). *Tarasoff and beyond* (Rev. ed.). Sarasota, FL: Professional Resource Press.

VandeCreek, L., & Knapp, S. (1997). Record keeping. In J. Matthews (Ed.), *Basic skills and professional issues in clinical psychology* (pp. 155–172). New York: Allyn & Bacon.

Van der Kolk, B. (1995). The body, memory, and the psychobiology of trauma. In J. Alpert (Ed.), *Sexual abuse recalled: Treating trauma in the era of the recovered memory debate* (pp. 29–60). Northvale, NJ: Aronson.

Williams, L. M. (1994). Recall of childhood trauma: A prospective study of women's memories of child sexual abuse. *Journal of Consulting and Clinical Psychology, 62,* 1167–1176.

Wilkinson v. Balsam, 885 F. Supp. 651 (D. Vt. 1995).

Wylie, M. S. (1993, October). The shadow of doubt. *The Family Therapy Networker, 17,* 18–30, 70, 73.

Yapko, M. (1994). *Suggestions of abuse.* New York: Simon & Shuster.

Zipkin v. Freeman, 436 S.W.2d 753 (1968).

Appendix A

Risk Management Checklist

1. Are you familiar with the literature on childhood abuse and forgotten memories of past traumas? Suggested references are Herman (1992) and Terr (1994).
2. Are you familiar with the phenomena of reconstructive memory and memory implantation? Suggested references are British Psychological Society (1995) and Loftus (1993).
3. Are you meticulous about maintaining appropriate therapeutic boundaries with your patients? Do you focus on your patient's psychological needs as opposed to public advocacy for a particular social issue?
4. Do you collaborate with patients in establishing treatment goals and keep open the possibility of alternative hypotheses concerning the origin of their problems?
5. Is your diagnostic procedure consistent with acceptable professional standards?
6. Do you refrain from using certain "high risk statements" listed in Appendix B which have the potential for misleading patients?
7. Are your treatment procedures based on scientifically or professionally derived principles?
8. Do you accept and explain the limitations of your techniques and abilities, despite the desire of some patients to attribute greater power to you than is warranted?
9. Do you avoid the use of certain techniques (age-regression therapy, hypnosis, sodium amytal interview-

ing, etc.) which are reportedly designed to retrieve lost memories of abuse, but which have little scientific support? A suggested reference for the use of hypnosis for memory retrieval is Hammond et al. (1994).

10. If you use techniques for memory recall, do your patients understand the limitations and potential for creating false memories associated with these memory retrieval techniques? Have you recorded what the patient recalled before the "de-repression" techniques were used? Do you audiotape or videotape the "de-repression" session? Are you aware of the iatrogenic possibilities of these techniques?

11. Do patients participate in establishing treatment goals? Do they understand the benefits and limitations of the techniques being used?

12. Do your treatment procedures show concern for the long-term impact on the patient, including future relationships with other family members?

13. Do you document your interventions thoroughly and carefully?

14. Do you seek consultation for difficult cases?

15. Do you carefully monitor the quality of care of those persons you supervise?

Appendix B

Statements That May Reflect Substandard Practices

1. "You have the symptoms of someone who was abused."

2. "Studies show that (or, My experience is that) most people with [fill in the particular diagnosis or symptoms here] were sexually abused."

3. "If you think you were abused, then you probably were."

4. "Remembering is essential if you want to be healed."

5. "This technique (hypnosis, guided imagery, sodium amytal, etc.) is designed to help you remember."

6. "Suing (Forgiving, Detaching from, etc.) your family is a necessary part of healing."

7. "You have to get worse before you get better."

8. "Your body holds accurate memories of past events."

Appendix C

Sample Informed Consent Form

My psychotherapist, _____ , has informed me, _____ , of the benefits and limitations of using _____ [hypnosis, age regression, etc.]

I have been informed that my psychotherapist is using [hypnosis, age regression, etc.] to

_____

_____

My psychotherapist has informed me that the perceptions or impressions uncovered under [hypnosis, age regression, etc.]

a. may not be accurate;
b. may be perceived as vivid and real, even if they did not occur; and
c. may be influenced by the method of presentation by the psychotherapist, my personal expectations, and other extraneous factors.

_____   _____
signature of patient   date

_____
signature of psychotherapist

Appendix D

Signals That May Suggest Distorted Memories

1. The patient reports a clear memory before the age of 2.
2. The patient has memories that are inconsistent with the developmental stage of the survivor at the time of the alleged abuse.
3. The patient reports events that have a low base rate (are bizarre or highly improbable).
4. The memories of the patient appear influenced by substandard previous therapy that included misleading hypnosis, a high pressure survivor group, or suggestive bibliotherapy.
5. The memories of the patient appear influenced by extra-therapeutic sources such as talk shows, popular books, or friends who are survivors.
6. The patient insists on hypnosis or other memory retrieval techniques to verify memories and dismisses the problems inherent in those methods to recover memories.
7. The patient is not willing to discuss unexplored areas unrelated to the alleged trauma.
8. The patient has secondary gains for claiming memories of abuse.

Appendix E

Statement by the American Psychiatric Association

This statement was approved by the Board of Trustees of the American Psychiatric Association on December 12, 1993.

Statement on Memories of Sexual Abuse

This *Statement* is in response to the growing concern regarding memories of sexual abuse. The rise in reports of documented cases of child sexual abuse has been accompanied by a rise in reports of sexual abuse that cannot be documented. Members of the public, as well as members of mental health and other professions, have debated the validity of some memories of sexual abuse, as well as some of the therapeutic techniques which have been used. The American Psychiatric Association has been concerned that the passionate debates about these issues have obscured the recognition of a body of scientific evidence that underlies widespread agreement among psychiatrists regarding psychiatric treatment in this area. We are especially concerned that the public confusion and dismay over this issue and the possibility of false accusations not discredit the reports of patients who have indeed been traumatized by actual previous abuse. While much more needs to be known, this *Statement* summarizes information about this topic that is important for psychiatrists in their work with patients for whom sexual abuse is an issue.

Sexual abuse of children and adolescents leads to severe negative consequences. Child sexual abuse is a risk factor for many classes of psychiatric disorders, including anxiety disorders, affective disorders, dissociative disorders and personality disorders.

Children and adolescents may be abused by family members, including parents and siblings, and by individuals outside of their families, including adults in trusted positions (e.g., teachers, clergy, camp counsellors). Abusers come from all walks of life. There is no uniform "profile" or other method to accurately distinguish those who have sexually abused children from those who have not.

Children and adolescents who have been abused cope with the trauma by using a variety of psychological mechanisms. In some instances, these coping mechanisms result in a lack of conscious awareness of the abuse for varying periods of time. Conscious thoughts and feelings stemming from the abuse may emerge at a later date.

It is not known how to distinguish, with complete accuracy, memories based on true events from those derived from other sources. The following observations have been made:

□ Human memory is a complex process about which there is a substantial base of scientific knowledge. Memory can be divided into four stages: Input (encoding), storage, retrieval, and recounting. All of these processes can be influenced by a variety of factors, including developmental stage, expectations and knowledge base prior to an event; stress and bodily sensations experienced during an event; post-event questioning; and the experience and context of the recounting of the event. In addition, the retrieval and recounting of a memory can modify the form of the memory, which may influence the content and the conviction about the veracity of the memory in the future. Scientific knowledge is not yet precise enough to predict how a certain experience or factor will influence a memory in a given person.

- Implicit and explicit memory are two different forms of memory that have been identified. *Explicit memory* (also termed declarative memory) refers to the ability to consciously recall facts or events. *Implicit memory* (also termed procedural memory) refers to behavioral knowledge of an experience without conscious recall. A child who demonstrates knowledge of a skill (e.g., bicycle riding) without recalling how he/she learned it, or an adult who has an affective reaction to an event without understanding the basis for that reaction (e.g., a combat veteran who panics when he hears the sound of a helicopter, but cannot remember that he was in a helicopter crash which killed his best friend) are demonstrating implicit memories in the absence of explicit recall. This distinction between explicit and implicit memory is fundamental because they have been shown to be supported by different brain systems, and because their differentiation and identification may have important clinical implications.
- Some individuals who have experienced documented traumatic events may nevertheless include some false or inconsistent elements in their reports. In addition, hesitancy in making a report, and recanting following the report can occur in victims of documented abuse. Therefore, these seemingly contradictory findings do not exclude the possibility that the report is based on a true event.
- Memories can be significantly influenced by questioning, especially in young children. Memories also can be significantly influenced by a trusted person (e.g., therapist, parent involved in a custody dispute) who suggests abuse as an explanation for symptoms/problems, despite initial lack of memory of such abuse. It has also been shown that repeated questioning may lead individuals to report "memories" of events that never occurred.

It is not known what proportion of adults who report memories of sexual abuse were actually abused. Many individuals who recover memories of abuse have been able to find corroborating information about their memories. However, no such information can be found, or is possible to obtain, in some situations. While aspects of the alleged abuse situation, as well as the context in which the memories emerge, can contribute to the assessment, there is no completely accurate way of determining the validity of reports in the absence of corroborating information.

Psychiatrists are often consulted in situations in which memories of sexual abuse are critical issues. Psychiatrists may be involved in a variety of capacities, including as the treating clinician for the alleged victim, for the alleged abuser, or for other family member(s); as a school consultant; or in a forensic capacity.

Basic clinical and ethical principles should guide the psychiatrist's work in this difficult area. These include the need for role clarity. It is essential that the psychiatrist and the other involved parties understand and agree on the psychiatrist's role.

Psychiatrists should maintain an empathic, non-judgmental, neutral stance towards reported memories of sexual abuse. As in the treatment of all patients, care must be taken to avoid prejudging the cause of the patient's difficulties, or the veracity of the patient's reports. A strong prior belief by the psychiatrist that sexual abuse, or other factors, are or are not the cause of the patient's problems is likely to interfere with appropriate assessment and treatment. Many individuals who have experienced sexual abuse have a history of not being believed by their parents, or others in whom they have put their trust. Expression of disbelief is likely to cause the patient further pain and decrease his/her willingness to seek needed psychiatric treatment. Similarly, clinicians should not exert pressure on patients to believe in events that may not have occurred, or to prematurely disrupt important relationships or make other important decisions based on these speculations. Clinicians who have not had the training necessary to evaluate and treat patients with a broad range of psychiatric disorders are at risk of causing harm by providing inadequate care for the patient's psychiatric problems and by increasing the patient's resistance to obtaining and responding to appropriate treatment in the future. In addition, special knowledge and experience are necessary to properly evaluate and/or treat patients who report the emergence of memories during the use of specialized interview techniques (e.g., the use of hypnosis or amytal), or during the course of litigation.

The treatment plan should be based on a complete psychiatric assessment, and should address the full range of the patient's clinical needs. In addition to specific treatments for any primary psychiatric condition, the patient may need help recognizing and integrating data that informs and defines the issues related to the memories of abuse. As in the treatment of patients with any psychiatric disorder, it may be important to caution the patient against making major life decisions during the acute phase of treatment. During the acute and later phases of treatment, the issues of breaking off relationships with important attachment figures, of pursuing legal actions, and of making public disclosures may need to be addressed. The psychiatrist should help the patient assess the likely impact (including emotional) of such decisions, given the patient's overall clinical and social situation. Some patients will be left with unclear memories of abuse and no corroborating information. Psychiatric treatment may help these patients adapt to the uncertainty regarding such emotionally important issues.

The intensity of public interest and debate about these topics should not influence psychiatrists to abandon their commitment to basic principles of ethical practice, delineated in *The Principles of Medical Ethics with Annotations Especially Applicable to Psychiatry*. The following concerns are of particular relevance:

- Psychiatrists should refrain from making public statements about the veracity or other features of individual reports of sexual abuse.
- Psychiatrists should vigilantly assess the impact of their conduct on the boundaries of the doctor/patient rela-

tionship. This is especially critical when treating patients who are seeking care for conditions that are associated with boundary violations in their past.

The APA [American Psychiatric Association] will continue to monitor developments in this area in an effort to help psychiatrists provide the best possible care for their patients.

Appendix F

Final Conclusions of the APA Working Group on Investigation of Memories of Childhood Abuse

In February 1993, the APA Council of Representatives established a working group to review current scientific literature and identify future research and training needs regarding the evaluation of memories of childhood abuse. The concluding section, reprinted here, summarizes the points of agreement and disagreement in the body of the full report and identifies future actions that should be taken. The complete final report with this concluding section was presented to the APA Board of Directors on February 14, 1996.

Final Conclusions of the APA Working Group on Investigation of Memories of Childhood Abuse

In this section, we seek to set a context for the following documents by summarizing our points of agreement and disagreement. We also articulate some of the implications of our deliberations for clinical practice, forensic practice, research,

From American Psychological Association *Working Group on the Investigation of Memories of Childhood Abuse: Final Report.* Alpert et al., (1996).

and training. Finally, we conclude with a plea for unity within our discipline.

Where Do We Stand?

Inspection of the following reviews and commentaries will indicate that we are in agreement concerning a number of key points. Indeed, as indicated in the Working Group's Interim Report, we agree on the following:

1. Controversies regarding adult recollections should not be allowed to obscure the fact that child sexual abuse is a complex and pervasive problem in America that has historically gone unacknowledged.

2. Most people who were sexually abused as children remember all or part of what happened to them.

3. It is possible for memories of abuse that have been forgotten for a long time to be remembered.

4. It is also possible to construct convincing pseudomemories for events that never occurred.

5. There are gaps in our knowledge about the processes that lead to accurate and inaccurate recollections of childhood abuse.

As important as these areas of agreement are, it is equally if not more important to acknowledge frankly that we differ markedly on a wide range of issues. At the core, the clinical and research subgroups have fundamentally differing views of the nature of memory. These contrasting conceptions of memory have led to debate concerning (a) the constructive nature of memory and the accuracy with which any events can be remembered over extended delays; (b) the tentative mechanisms that may underlie delayed remembering; (c) the presumed "special" status of memories of traumatic events; (d) the relevance of the basic memory and developmental literatures for understanding the recall of stressful events; (e) the rules of evidence by which we can test hypotheses about the consequences of trauma and the nature of remembering; (f) the frequency with which pseudomemories may be created by suggestion, both within and outside of therapy; and (g) the ease with which, in the absence of external corroborative evidence, "real" and pseudomemories may be distinguished.

Where Do We Go?

Given this characterization of our understanding of the critical issues, how do we proceed from here? And what are the implications of these documents for research, practice, training, and forensic psychology? As suggested above, one of the most consistent observations emerging from our deliberations has to do with the very divergent epistemologies and definitions utilized by psychologists who study memory and those who study and treat effects of trauma. Although there are exceptions, we frequently do not speak the same professional language or define phenomena in the same manner; we read different journals and books, and attend different specialty meetings; and each group finds useful and compelling studies that the other group sees as problematic and questionable. Many of the difficulties that we have encountered in attempting to achieve consensus reflect these profound epistemological differences, a phenomenon which has been previously documented in studies comparing psychological scientists and psychological practitioners (Kalinkowitz, 1978; Caddy, 1981; Dawes, 1994). If we are to go forward toward the development of productive research that will be found to be credible by both scientists and practitioners, and toward the promotion of clinical practice that is truly rooted in psychological science, some steps must be taken to resolve these epistemological differences and develop consensual definitions about what is being studied and discussed.

To begin, it is essential to address fundamental differences between the two subgroups in terms of basic definitions of the issues under investigation. Thus, for example, it is necessary to consider the two groups' contrasting views of the nature of early trauma and the young child's representation of various types of sexual abuse. Accordingly, one important implication of our deliberations is that psychologists who work in the field of trauma and those who study memory would benefit from working collaboratively to (a) develop paradigms for research; (b) search for consensual definitions of constructs that speak to the issue of how trauma affects memory; and (c) develop models that will be scientifically sound while being well-grounded in the realities of clinical practice. No matter how well designed, a study that equates stressful experiences that are socially sanctioned with those involving pain, betrayal and loss of safety will be found less credible by those who treat the survivors of the latter, just as texts on treatment, no matter how therapeutically useful they may seem based on the author's anecdotal observations, will lack credibility to scientists when what is clinically suggested violates the data available through research.

Some studies of therapists (Yapko, 1994; Poole, Lindsay, Memon, & Bull, 1995) have criticized practitioners for their lack of knowledge of the workings of memory and their willingness to endorse techniques that might implant suggestions. An alternative view of this state of affairs might be that based on their experience, which is a powerful source of data for practicing clinicians, many therapists have developed beliefs about techniques that they feel are clinically effective in reducing the distress of trauma survivors. Future research is needed to evaluate the validity of these beliefs and to better inform both practitioners and researchers as to the characterization of "useful" as opposed to "risky" approaches to interventions.

The epistemological foundation from which one evaluates clinical outcomes or research findings affects the meaning given to those outcomes/findings. Because the entire Working Group converges on the belief that science-informed practice will be the most effective strategy for treatment, we believe that practice-informed research will enhance the integration of knowledge about memory into the overall field of trauma treatment. This direction in research may also help us to answer the still unclear questions about the nature of various observed human behaviors in response to trauma.

Implications for Practice

The deliberations of the Working Group strongly underscore the importance of a careful and science-based preparation for professional practice in psychology. Many possible errors in working with adult survivors, or with clients who present as recovering memories of childhood abuse, could be avoided if the therapist were well-grounded in developmental psychology (particularly developmental psychopathology and cognitive development), cognitive psychology (especially the study of memory), and research on trauma (with an emphasis on the range of responses to interpersonal violence). Both the scientist–practitioner (PhD) and scholar–practitioner (PsyD) models of training embrace this necessity. Given the very high rates of histories of some kinds of interpersonal violence among the patient population (Jacobson & Richardson, 1987), all doctoral level training programs in professional psychology, including those whose primary focus is the training of clinical researchers, should insure that students are exposed to formal course work and supervised practica in which the role of interpersonal violence as a risk factor for psychopathology is central. Currently practicing psychologists, if lacking in these knowledge bases, should be encouraged to pursue formal continuing professional education on these topics. Care should be taken to insure that instructors (and course curricula) reflect a science knowledge base as well as high-quality clinical practice.

A second important implication of our findings for clinical practice is that *care, caution, and consistency* should be utilized in working with any client, and particularly one who experiences what is believed (by either client or therapist) to be a recovered memory of trauma. Moreover, clients in all circumstances must be given information about possible treatment strategies and should in turn provide *informed consent* for treatment. As with any intervention, clients have the right to know both risks and benefits of procedures used by a therapist. Careful histories should be taken from all clients, and questions about the entire range of risk factors, including but not limited to a history of sexual abuse, must be asked of all new clients, not only those whose symptoms arouse suspicions of abuse in a clinician. This is because such suspicion may be unfounded, while genuine experiences of interpersonal violence may never be volunteered by clients with such histories whose symptoms do not conform to a clinician's beliefs about the sequelae of abuse. Questions should be phrased in a non-leading manner, and in the most open-ended way possible, in order to promote a more behaviorally descriptive and less affectively-laden introduction of this difficult topic into the history-taking process.

When clients report what they phenomenologically experience as memories of previously unrecollected trauma, therapists should take a number of steps to avoid imposing a particular version of reality on these experiences and to reduce risks of the creation of pseudomemories. If these materials are intrusive and create problems for the client's functioning, the first goal of treatment should be stabilization and containment following the recommendations of many experts in the field of trauma treatment. It is important to remember that the goal of therapy is not archeology; recollection of trauma is only helpful insofar as it is integrated into a therapy emphasizing improvement of functioning. Therapists should avoid endorsing such retrievals as either clearly truthful or clearly confabulated. Instead, the focus should be on aiding the client in developing his or her own sense of what is real and truthful. Clients can be encouraged to search for information that would add to their ability to find themselves credible (e.g., contemporaneous writings, reports of third parties), and to carefully weigh the evidence. Therapists should carefully consider all alternative hypotheses, including: (a) that the retrieved material is a reasonably accurate memory of real events; (b) that it is a distorted memory of real events, with distortions due to developmental factors or source contaminations; (c) that it is a confabulation emerging from underlying psychopathology or difficulties with reality testing; (d) that it is a pseudomemory emerging from exposure to suggestions; or (e) that it is a form of self-suggestion emerging from the client's internal suggestive mechanisms.

Clients who seek hypnosis as a means of retrieving or confirming their recollections should be advised that it is not an appropriate procedure for this goal because of the serious risk that pseudomemories may be created in trance states and of the related risk due to increased confidence in those memories. Clients should also be informed that the use of hypnosis could jeopardize any future legal actions they might wish to take. Moreover, in those situations in which hypnosis is employed, it is necessary to interpret the client's responses in light of parallel measures of suggestibility and proneness to fantasy.

As indicated above, it can be helpful to seek corroborative evidence for claims of sexual abuse. Nonetheless, denials by alleged perpetrators should also not be taken as evidence that the client is experiencing other than an accurate recollection. Indeed, known perpetrators of child sexual abuse can also deny and lie about their behaviors, even in the presence of physical evidence that incontrovertibly links them to the abuse, and sometimes tell their victims that the abuse "never happened" or should be forgotten. Finally, while there are no statistics available on its prevalence, it is known that on occasion adults who report recovering memories will lie, particularly when the constellation of motives (fear, embarrassment, desire to protect loved ones, desire for revenge) outweigh the incentives to tell the truth.

In some states, persons who have recovered memories of childhood sexual abuse are eligible for crime victims' compensation if they report the alleged abuse to the police in a timely fashion. They are then treated as any other victims/witnesses of a crime. When resources for treatment are in short supply, this course may be attractive to both client and therapist as a means of insuring payment for therapy. However, both parties need to be especially cautious in making assertions to legal authorities as to the factual basis of recent recollections. Such actions may prematurely commit both therapist and client to a particular interpretation of the information reported by the client, and may commit a client in some instances to testifying in a resulting criminal case, should the report fall within statutory limits. Thus, therapists should explore a variety of other alternatives with the client before embarking on this particular course.

In short, a responsible path for therapists to pursue is one in which clients are empowered to be the authority about their own lives and reality, where the emphasis is on recovery and function, and where memories of trauma are viewed within the context of what one might tentatively assume to be a post-traumatic response. This approach, however, may mean that clients occasionally reach conclusions about what may have happened to them that we find difficult to accept. Nonetheless, respect for the dignity of adults who seek treatment must inevitably temper therapists' efforts at reality testing. Therapists need to eschew the roles of advocate, detective, or ultimate arbiter of reality, unless the veracity of the material being constructed/retrieved becomes important for either therapeutic or legal reasons.

Implications for Forensic Practitioners

The role of the forensic psychologist is that of an educator to the triers of fact, the judge and jury. In that capacity, forensic psychologists, in general, should avoid attempting to speak to the ultimate issue (i.e., guilt or innocence) in a case, because they usually are not in a position to know the truth. Forensic psychologists should always exercise caution, temper the degree of certainty with which they offer their testimony, and be aware of both the problems and the strengths of their methodologies. How then, can forensic experts practice responsibly in cases where questions of recovered memories of childhood abuse are involved?

First, whenever possible, therapists should avoid serving as expert forensic witnesses in the cases involving clients whom they are treating. This is consistent with APA ethical standards, and with guidelines published by the Division 41 of APA (Psychology and Law—AP/LS) for forensic practice. Experts, moreover, should confine their testimony to their specific areas of expertise and knowledge. For example, questions of the appropriate standard of care would ordinarily be the purview of those trained in the fields of professional psychology; this might be distinguished from expert testimony about risks of a specific therapeutic technique when the technique or practice being considered is one in which scientists' findings could be applicable (e.g., the risks of using hypnosis to bolster a memory). When evaluating a person who alleges having recalled memories of childhood abuse, forensic experts should utilize all possible sources of information, and not rely solely upon the self-report of either plaintiff or defendant. Possible sources of suggestion and contamination should be explored rigorously. Because there is no one syndrome or symptom pattern associated with a history of childhood sexual abuse, care should be utilized in making inferences from the symptoms to the credibility of a plaintiff's report.

In cases involving complaints against therapists who are alleged to have created pseudomemories of sexual abuse, similar care should be taken by forensic psychologists to rely on a variety of sources of information and to search for the convergent validity of data. Reports by clients of what has occurred in therapy may or may not be accurate; reports by therapists about what transpired in therapy may or may not be accurate; and reports by third parties who were not present at the treatment may or may not be accurate. When feasible, expert clinical opinions should be based upon direct or videotaped observation, and not simply reviews of written or audiotaped materials.

Implications for Research and Training

Just as the Working Group has endorsed the value of a [scientifically-informed approach to practice], its members also endorse the value of a [practice-informed approach to research]. There is much to be gained by both researchers and practitioners when their respective insights cross-fertilize each other's professional activities.

For researchers, this means incorporating into their designs as many of the ingredients of real-world trauma as is ethically and practically permissible, and learning from clinicians about those phenomena that require further study. In this regard, in recent years there has developed a large body of naturalistic empirical research that stands at the interface between the domains of memory and trauma. Examples include Wagenaar and Groeneweg's (1990) study of Dutch concentration camp survivors' memories of victimization; Parker, Bahrick, Lundy, Fivush, and Levitt's (1995) study of child survivors of Hurricane Andrew; both Merritt, Ornstein, and Spicker's (1994) and Goodman, Quas, Batterman-Fraunce, Riddlesberger, and Kuhn's (1994) explorations of children's bladder catheterization; and Eisen, Goodman, and Qin's (1995) study of the susceptibility of sexually abused children to sexual suggestions. More recently, there have also been studies of the neurobiological substrates of memory for traumatic events (Bremer et al., 1995; Yehuda et al., 1995). Nonetheless, there is a clear need for more of this sort of research, particularly as it applies to the phenomenon of repetitive boundary violations within the family setting, in which a number of complex person-situation variables are at play.

For practice-oriented students, cross-fertilization means that training faculty need to insure that they are well grounded not only in the substance of scientific psychology but also in its core values (e.g., the pursuit of "proof by disproof" as the strongest means of knowing). For research-oriented students, this means some degree of orientation to the limitations of generalizability of research findings to clinical applications, and a familiarity with clinically observed phenomena that require further study. In an ideal world, all graduate trainees, whether in practice or scientific research, would be exposed to each other's ideas, readings, and experiences, and would thus acquire a common vocabulary and shared knowledge base.

Too often, members of each group develop in what amounts to a culture of isolation from the other group's knowledge and experiences. To some extent, this is the unhappy consequence of increased specialization and the need for increasingly prolonged and focused apprenticeships to acquire the tools of each of these psychological trades. Presently, the sheer amount of domain-specific knowledge that must be learned to be considered competent in science or practice is enormous, and enjoinders to learn even more may seem unrealistic in view of the real limits of time and resources. Fortunately, there are ways of solving this dilemma that can expose each group to phenomena without requiring additional curricula, but merely a reorganization of what is already in place in many programs. What we have in mind is the use of critical case studies in training that bridge both groups' interest.

As an example, the issue before us—the recovered memory debate—is a window through which the generic chasm can be bridged. Both clinical and research trainees can be exposed to the type of argument and data contained in this Working Group Report as a means of not only acquainting them with the specifics of this particular debate, but far more importantly of inculcating a sense that the world is full of phenomena that require a consideration of both groups' perspectives. Clinical students, as well as those studying both cognitive and developmental psychology, would benefit from a consideration of the issues that have animated this debate, and it could be couched in the context of existing course work.

This case study approach, moreover, can also serve to teach valuable lessons about professional behaviors that are and are not consistent with standards of good practice or good science. From our perspective, there are signs everywhere of psychologists making public pronouncements on matters of importance, based on anecdotes and impressions rather than on systematic empirical evidence, challenged by alternative explanations. When researchers and clinicians espouse views in public, including courtrooms, they have the highest responsibility to make clear to their audiences the limits to generalization of their conclusions, all known threats to the external validity of their information-gathering procedures and/or clinical interpretations, and the results of attempts to test alternative explanations. These professional behaviors can be illustrated readily in the context of this and other important debates.

A Final Statement

We wish to end on a note with which we can all agree. The members of the Working Group, individually and collectively, bemoan the increasing "Balkanization" of psychology, a development that has surely made our tasks more difficult as we have attempted to bridge across powerful gaps of understanding. Our discipline has spawned many psychologies, often disconnected from each other, and both the cortical and ethical glues that ought to have connected them seem to have been neglected. We are fast becoming a collection of psychologies, each uninformed by the data and epistemologies of the others; in short, we are pluribus, but not unum. And most critically, we need to change dramatically if psychology as a discipline seeks to lead the way in avoiding harm to all those who are affected by the consequences of both accurate and false recollections of abuse.

References

Bremer, J. D., Randall, P., Scott, T. M., Bronen, R. A., Seibyl, J. P., Southwick, S. M., Delaney, R. C., McCarthy, G., Charney, D. S., & Innis, R. B. (1995). MRI-based measurement of hippocampal volume in patients with combat-related posttraumatic stress disorder. *American Journal of Psychiatry, 152,* 973–981.

Caddy, G. R. (1981, June). The development and current status of professional psychology. *Professional Psychology, 12*(3), 377–384.

Dawes, R. M. (1994). *House of cards: Psychology and psychotherapy built on myth.* New York: Free Press.

Eisen, M. L., Goodman, G. S., & Qin, J. (1995, May). *The impact of dissociation and stress arousal on the suggestibility and memory of abused or neglected children.* In F. J. Morrison (Moderator), *Children's memory: Implications for Testimony.* Invited symposium at the meetings of the Midwestern Psychological Association, Chicago.

Goodman, G. S., Quas, J. A., Batterman-Faunce, J. M., Riddlesberger, M. M., & Kuhn, J. (1994). Predictors of accurate and inaccurate memories of traumatic events experienced in childhood. *Consciousness and Cognition, 3,* 269–294.

Jacobson, A., & Richardson, B. C. (1987). Assault experiences of 100 psychiatric inpatients: Evidence of the need for routine inquiry. *American Journal of Psychiatry, 144,* 434–440.

Kalinkowitz, B. (1978, Fall). Scientist-practitioner: the widening schism. *Clinical Psychologist, 32*(1), 4–5.

Merritt, K. A., Ornstein, P. A., & Spicker, B. (1994). Children's memory of a salient medical procedure: Implications for testimony. *Pediatrics, 94,* 17–23.

Parker, J. F., Bahrick, L. E., Lundy, B., Fivush, R., & Levitt, M. J. (1995, July). *Children's memory for a natural disaster: Effects of stress.* In Parker, J. (Moderator), *Eyewitness memory: Effects of stress and arousal upon children's memories.* Symposium at the meetings of the Society for Applied Research in Memory and Cognition, Vancouver, BC.

Appendix G

Statement by the British Psychological Society

Overall Conclusions

□ Normal event memory is largely accurate but may contain distortions and elaborations.

□ With certain exceptions, such as where there has been extensive rehearsal of an imagined event, the source of our memories is generally perceived accurately.

□ Nothing can be recalled accurately from before the first birthday and little from before the second. Poor memory from before the fourth birthday is normal.

□ Forgetting of certain kinds of trauma is often reported, although the nature of the mechanism or mechanisms involved remains unclear.

□ While there is a great deal of evidence for incorrect memories, there is currently much less evidence on the creation of false memories.

□ Hypnosis makes memory more confident and less reliable. It can also be used to create amnesia for events.

□ There are a number of significant differences between false confessions and false (recovered) memories which preclude generalising from one to the other.

□ There are high levels of belief in the essential accuracy of recovered memories of child sexual abuse among qualified psychologists. These beliefs appear to be fuelled by the high levels of experience of recovered memories both for CSA and for non-CSA traumatic events. The non-doctrinaire nature of these beliefs is indicated by the high level of acceptance of the possibility of false memories.

□ There is not a lot of evidence that accusers fit a single profile. From the British records, at least, there is no good evidence that accusers have invariably recovered memories from total amnesia. Further documentation of the phenomenon is needed by the False Memory societies in order to obtain a more reliable picture. It appears that only in a small minority of instances do the accusations concern abuse that ended before the age of five.

□ Guidelines can be laid down for good practice in therapy.

Recommendations

1. We recommend that the Society use all means available to ensure that Chartered Psychologists who carry out therapy do so in accordance with our guidelines.

2. We recommend that BPS approved training courses in psychological therapies should include appropriate information concerning the properties of human memory.

3. We recommend that the Royal Colleges of Psychiatrists, Nursing and General Practice, and the psychotherapy training organisations affiliated to the United Kingdom Council for Psychotherapy and the British Confederation of Psychotherapists should initiate action equivalent to 1. and 2. above.

4. We recommend that the Department of Health, Medical Research Council and Economic and Social Research Council give increased priority to research in the areas covered in this report, particularly those which integrate cognitive and clinical approaches. Examples include naturalistic studies of recovered memory, basic research on inhibitory processes of memory and beliefs and practices in psychotherapy.

5. We recommend that the Department of Health take our findings into consideration in their review of NHS psycho-

therapy services, in relation to the quality of psychotherapy services and training.

6. We recommend that the Society and the Department of Health bring appropriate parts of our report to the attention of the general public to enable therapy clients to evaluate the conceptual and scientific basis of alternative therapies.

Appendix H

The Australian Psychological Society Limited Code of Professional Conduct and Guidelines Relating to Recovered Memories

A. Code of Professional Conduct

The Australian Psychological Society Code of Professional Conduct sets forth principles of professional conduct designed to safeguard

- the welfare of consumers of psychological services
- the integrity of the profession

The General Principles of the Code are:

I. Responsibility

Psychologists remain personally responsible for the professional decisions they take

- Psychologists are expected to take cognisance of the foreseeable consequences of their actions and to make every effort to ensure that their services are used appropriately.
- In working with organisations, whether as employees or consultants, psychologists shall have ultimate regard for the highest standards of their profession.

II. Competence

Psychologists shall bring to and maintain appropriate skills and learning in their areas of professional practice

- Psychologists must not misrepresent their competence, qualifications, training or experience.
- Psychologists shall refrain from offering or undertaking work or advice beyond their professional competence.

III. Propriety

The welfare of clients, students, research participants and the public, and the integrity of the profession, shall take precedence over a psychologist's self-interest and over the interests of the psychologist's employer and colleagues.

- Psychologists must respect the confidentiality of information obtained from persons in the course of their work as psychologists. They may reveal such information to others only with the consent of the person or the person's legal representative, except in those unusual circumstances in which not to do so would result in clear danger to the person or to others. Psychologists must inform their clients of the legal or other contractual limits of confidentiality.
- Psychologists shall refrain from any act which would tend to bring the profession into public disrepute.

B. Guidelines Relating to Recovered Memories

These Guidelines set forth conclusions and recommendations designed to safeguard psychologists and clients who are dealing with reports of recovered memories.

I. Scientific Issues

Memory is a constructive and reconstructive process. What is remembered about an event is shaped by what was observed of that event, by conditions prevailing during attempts to remember, and by events occurring between the observation and the attempted remembering. Memories can be altered, deleted, and created by events that occur during and after the time of encoding, and during the period of storage, and during any attempts at retrieval.

Memory is integral to many approaches to therapy. Repression and dissociation are processes central to some theories and approaches to therapy. According to these theories and approaches, memories of traumatic events may be blocked out unconsciously and this leads to a person having no memory of the events. However, memories of these traumatic events may become accessible at some later time. Although some clinical observations support the notion of repressed memories, empirical research on memories generally does not. Moreover the scientific evidence does not allow general statements to be made about any relationship between trauma and memory.

"Memories" that are reported either spontaneously or following the use of special procedures in therapy may be accurate, inaccurate, fabricated, or a mixture of these. The level of belief in memory or the emotion associated with the memory does not predict the accuracy of the memory. The available scientific and clinical evidence does not allow accurate, inaccurate, and fabricated memories to be distinguished in the absence of independent corroboration.

Psychologists should recognise that reports of abuse long

after the alleged events are difficult to prove or disprove in the majority of cases. Independent corroboration of the statements of those who make or deny such allegations is typically difficult, if not impossible. Accordingly, psychologists should exercise special care in dealing with clients, their family members, and the wider community when allegations of past abuse are made.

II. Clinical Issues

Psychologists should evaluate critically their assumptions or biases about attempts to recover memories of trauma-related events. Equally, psychologists should assist clients to understand any assumptions that they have about repressed or recovered memories. Assumptions that adult problems may or may not be associated with repressed memories from childhood can not be sustained by available scientific evidence.

Psychologists should be alert to the ways that they can shape the memories reported by clients through the expectations they convey, the comments they make, the questions they ask, and the responses they give to clients. Psychologists should be alert that clients are susceptible to subtle suggestions and reinforcements, whether those communications are intended or unintended. Therefore, psychologists should record intact memories at the beginning of therapy, and be aware of any possible contagion effects (e.g., self-help groups, popular books).

Psychologists should be alert to the role that they may play in creating or shaping false memories. Equally, psychologists should be alert not to dismiss memories that may be based in fact. At all times, psychologists should be empathic and supportive of the reports of clients while also ensuring that clients do not jump to conclusions about the truth or falsity of their recollections of the past. They should also ensure that alternative causes of any problems that are reported are explored. Psychologists should recognise that the context of therapy is important as is the content.

Psychologists should not avoid asking clients about the possibility of sexual or other abusive occurrences in their past, if such a question is relevant to the problem being treated. However, psychologists should be cautious in interpreting the response that is given. Psychologists should never assume that a report of no abuse is necessarily indicative of either repressed or dissociated memory or denial of known events. Nor should they assume that a report of abuse indicates necessarily that the client was abused.

Psychologists should understand clearly the difference between narrative truth and historical truth, and the relevance of this difference inside the therapy context and outside that context. Memory reports as part of a personal narrative can be helpful in therapy independent of the accuracy of those reports. However, to be accepted as actual history, those reports should be shown to be accurate. Psychologists should seek to meet the needs of clients who report memories of abuse, and should do this quite apart from the truth or falsity of those reports. Psychologists should recognize that the needs and well-being of clients take precedence and should design their therapeutic interventions accordingly.

III. Ethical Issues

Psychologists treating clients who report recovered memories of abuse are expected to observe the Principles set out in the Code of Professional Conduct of the Australian Psychological Society, and in the Code of Professional Conduct of the Psychologists' Registrations Boards in States in which they are registered as psychologists. Specifically, psychologists should obtain informed consent at the beginning of therapy in relation to the details of the therapeutic process and its possible consequences.

Psychologists should inform any client who recovers a memory of abuse that it may be an accurate memory of an actual event, may be an altered or distorted memory of an actual event, or may be a false memory of an event that did not happen. Psychologists should explore with the client the meaning and implications of the memory for the client, rather than focus solely on the content of the reported memory. Psychologists should explore with the client ways of determining the accuracy of the memory, if appropriate.

Psychologists should be alert particularly to the need to maintain appropriate skills and learning in this area, and should be aware of the relevant scientific evidence and clinical standards of practice. Psychologists should guard against accepting approaches to abuse and therapy that are not based in scientific evidence and appropriate clinical standards. Psychologists should be alert also to the personal responsibility they hold for the foreseeable consequence of their actions.

IV. Legal Issues

Psychologists should be aware that some approaches and writings concerning abuse and recovered memories urge clients to engage in legal action against the alleged abuser and any others who may question the accuracy of any recovered memories. Psychologists should recognize that their responsibilities are to the therapeutic needs of clients, and not to issues of legal action or revenge. Given that the accuracy of memories cannot be determined without corroboration, psychologists should use caution in responding to questions from clients about legal action.

Psychologists should be aware that their knowledge, skills, and practices may come under close scrutiny by various public and private agencies if they are treating clients who recover memories of abuse. Psychologists should ensure that comprehensive records are maintained about their sessions with clients who recover memories of abuse.

Psychologists should in no way tolerate, or be seen to tolerate, childhood or adult sexual abuse, or abuse of any kind. They should ensure that their psychological services are used appropriately in this regard, and should be alert to problems of deciding whether allegations of abuse are true or false. They should be alert especially to the different demands and processes of the therapeutic and legal contexts in dealing with such allegations.

V. Research Issues

Psychologists should be aware that research is needed to understand more about trauma-related memory, techniques to enhance memory, and techniques to deal effectively with childhood sexual abuse. Psychologists should support and contribute to research on these, and related, issues whenever possible.

Author Index

Abhold, 43
Abrams, 45
Alabama Supreme Court, 20
Alpert, J., 12, 34, 36, 45, 57, 58, 61
American Psychiatric Asociation, 58, 71, 72, 108, 118, 153
American Psychological Association, 1, 47, 48, 51, 53, 56, 60, 68, 69, 77, 88, 94, 121–123, 132, 159
Anderson, J., 49
Andrews v. United States, 117
Australian Psychological Society, 92, 177

Bahrick, L. E., 168
Barden, C., 3
Bass, E., 15, 37, 50, 52, 53, 56, 59, 93, 96
Batterman-Faunce, J. M., 168
Becker, J., 58, 76
Berger, K. S., 1
Berliner, L., 4
Bernardin Case, 126
Beutler, L., 58
Billings, F. J., 42
Bird, v. W.C.W., 20
Bloom, P., 56, 92
Bongar, B., 115
Bottoms, 104
Bremer, J. D., 168
Briere, J., 2, 5, 39, 70, 71, 73, 79, 83
British Psychological Society, 1, 37, 41, 58, 145, 173
Brown, L., 17, 36, 45, 49, 54, 58, 60, 61, 71, 78, 86, 91
Bull, R., 16, 162
Burgess, C., 78, 91

Burgess, M. F., 78, 91
Butler, K., 3
Byrd, I., 80

Caddy, G. R., 161
Canterbury v. Spence, 89
Caudill, O. B., 3, 13, 21, 99
Ceci, S. J., 35, 36
Chiu, S., 62
Ciocca, M., 123
Clayton, S., 115
Clevenger, N., 18
Clute, S., 96
Cobb v. Grant, 89
Conte, J., 39
Coons, P., 104
Cordes-Green, S., 87
Cosgrove v. Lawrence, 117
"Couple Brings Suit ...", 26
Courtois, C., 36, 45, 58, 61
Cruz-Lat, E., 13, 79, 84

Davis, L., 15, 37, 50, 52, 53, 56, 59, 93, 96
Dawes, R. M., 161
Dewhirst, B., 42
Donaldson, M. A., 87
DuBreuil, S., 42
Dzubia-Leatherman, J., 58

Einbinder, R. G., 95
Eisen, M. L., 168
Elliott, D. M., 2, 39
Emory University, v. Porubiansky, 117

Faigman, D., 18
False Memory Syndrome Foundation, 3, 24

Family Survey Update, 45, 102
Farmer, K., 4, 27, 28, 72, 73, 81, 87, 105
Feldman-Summers, S., 2, 39
Fetkewicz, J., 28, 59, 72, 93
Finkelhor, D., 58
Fivush, R., 168
Follette, V., 40, 54, 57, 60, 64, 114, 119
Fox, R., 2
Fredrickson, R., 52, 53, 56, 94
Freeland, A., 62
Freyd, J., 40
Freyd, P., 101
Fullilove, M., 39

Gabora, N., 42
Galanter, M., 87
"Girl recants tales . . .", 21, 26
Gold, S. N., 39, 82, 83
Goldberg, C., 114
Goldstein, E., 4, 27, 28, 72, 73, 81, 87, 105
Goodman, G. S., 168
Grinker, R., 38
Groeneweg, 168
Guthiel, T., 56, 97

Hamanne v. Humenansky, 25, 61, 70
Hammond, D. C., 91, 146
Harrar, W., 8, 117
Harsch, N., 42
Harvey, M. R., 57
Hashtroudi, S., 42
Helling v. Carey, 25
Herbison, G. P., 49
Herman, J., 39, 80, 82–87, 93, 145
Herman, J. L., 57
Hill, E., 58
Hinnefeld, B., 124, 125
Hintzman, D., 33
Hohnecker, L., 39, 82, 83
Hughes, D., 39, 61, 82, 83

Husband, R., 42
Hyman, I., 42

Jablonski v. United States, 111
Jacobson, A., 163
Johns Hopkins Medical Center, 3, 24
Johnson, M., 42
Johnson v. Johnson, 16
Jorgenson, P., 69
Joyce-Couch v. DeSilva, 25

Kalinkowitz, B., 161
Keck, P., 59
Keenan, M., 61
Ketcham, K., 27, 49, 51
Khatian v. Jones, 23, 99
Kluft, R. P., 56
Knapp, S., 8, 19, 48, 59, 107, 111, 117
Kramer, S., 61
Kuhn, J., 168

Lanning, K., 103
Latz, T., 61
Laurence, J. R., 41
Lee, S., 58
"Legal Actions Against Parents," 16
Levitt, M. J., 168
Lief, H., 28, 59, 72, 93
Lindsay, D. S., 2, 16, 41, 43, 78, 102, 126, 162
Lindsay, S., 42
Lipinski, J. F., 59
Loftus, E., 4, 27, 37, 39, 41, 49, 51, 53, 145
Loftus, E. F., 35, 36
Lohr, N., 58
London, R., 97
Lundy, B., 168

Maker, E., 95

"Malpractice lawsuit against therapist settles," 26
Maltsberger, J., 111
Maltz, W., 50
Manchanda, R., 62
Marine, E., 13, 21
Martin, J., 49
Martinez-Taboas, A., 38
Mayer, R., 73
McElroy, S., 59
McHugh, P., 62
McMillen, C., 58
McMinn, M., 104, 126, 127
McNamara, E., 52, 67, 88
McNulty, C., 96
Memon, A., 16, 162
Menary, E., 42
Merritt, K. A., 168
Merskey, H., 62
Montoya v. Bebensee, 20, 117
Mullen, P., 49
"My Sister's Story," 28

Nader, K., 43
Nagy, T., 90, 92
Nash, M., 80, 81
National Association for Consumer Protection in Mental Health Practices, 119, 133
Neisser, U., 42
Nelson, E., 27, 28, 78, 86

O'Connell, D. N., 80
Oksana, C., 76, 81
Orne, M. T., 80
Ornstein, P. A., 35, 36, 168
Osheroff v. Chestnut Hill Lodge, 67
Overstreet, S., 55

Paddison, P., 95
"Parents, Siblings Join Retractor in Lawsuit," 105
Parker, J., 103

Parker, J. F., 168
Pendergast, M., 4, 27, 28, 51, 52, 55, 70, 71, 95, 101, 103
Penfield, W., 32
Perry, C., 41
Polonksy, S., 39
Polusny, M., 40, 54, 57, 60, 64, 114, 119
Poole, D. A., 16, 54, 62, 93, 96, 104, 162
Poor, E., 88
Pope, H. G., 59
Pope, K., 1, 2, 17, 24, 39, 40, 45, 49, 54, 60, 64, 71, 78, 86, 91, 96
Prosser, W., 14
Pynoos, R. S., 43

Qin, J., 168
Quas, J. A., 168

Read, D., 2, 41, 43, 78, 102, 126
"Repressed Memory Claims Expected to Soar," 3
"Research Notes," 126, 127
Reviere, S. L., 84
Richardson, B. C., 163
Riddlesberger, M. M., 168
Rideout, G., 58
Rogers, M., 86
Romans, S., 49
Rosen, G., 97
Ross, A., 103
Rubin, L., 45

Salter, A., 52
Scanlon, 55
Schacter, D., 40
Schatzow, E., 39
Scheflin, A., 18, 78
Schneider, J., 21, 75
Schwarz, R., 55
Seligman, M., 126, 127
Shapiro, J., 18, 78
Sharma, V., 62

Sheiman, J. A., 39
Shor, R. E., 80
Silk, K., 58
Simon, R., 7, 14
Simpson, P., 27, 28, 78, 86
Soisson, E. L., 111
Spanos, N., 42, 78, 91
Spicker, B., 168
Spiegel, H., 38
State of New Hampshire House
    Bill 236, 121
State of New Hampshire v. Hunger-
    ford, 18
State of New Hampshire v. Morahan,
    18
Strain, J. J., 95
Strassburger, L., 69
"Suits against abusive therapists
    settled," 13, 26–28
Sullivan v. Cheshier, 22
Sutherland, P., 69

Tabachnick, B., 1, 40, 45, 64, 96
Tarasoff v. The Regents of the Uni-
versity of California et al., 19,
    123
Terr, L., 57, 82, 95, 109, 145
Thompson, R., 1
Tuman v. Genesis, 22

VandeCreek, L., 8, 19, 48, 59, 107,
    111, 117
Van der Kolk, B., 40
Vardi, 38

Wade, N., 104, 126, 127
Wagenaar, 168
Wardle, J., 96
Wilkinson v. Balsam, 20
Williams, L. M., 2, 39
Williams, R., 58
Wylie, M. S., 28

Yapko, M., 37, 51, 162
Yehuda, 168

Zetzer, H., 58
Zipkin v. Freeman, 70
Zuravin, S., 58

Subject Index

Abuse
frequency of, 1
harm vs. benefit from, 58–59
identification of past, 49–50
and later psychopathology, 57–60
memory of. *See* Memory of abuse
overemphasis on denial of, 54–56
overidentification of past, 50–56
overly broad definitions of, 51–52
Acceptable standards of care. *See* Standards of care
Adult children
lawsuits initiated by, against parents, 16–19
third-party lawsuits with, 20–23
Age regression, 80–81
Alabama, 20
Allegations of abuse, responses to, 4
Alpert, J., 12
Alternative techniques. *See* Unproven techniques
"Althaus case," 21, 25–26
American Association of Christian Counselors, 104
American Professional Agency, 3
American Psychiatric Association, 71, 72
Statement on Memories of Sexual Abuse, 153–158
American Psychological Association (APA)
Ethical Principles of Psychologists and Code of Conduct of, 47–48, 69, 88–89, 94, 121–123
Ethics Office of, 8, 9
Working Group on Investigation of Childhood Memories of Abuse, 45, 57, 159–170
Working Group on the Retrieval of Childhood Memories of Abuse, 34
American Society of Clinical Hypnosis, 91
Amnesia, 38, 40
infant, 101–102
Andrews v. United States, 117
APA. *See* American Psychological Association
Australian Psychological Society, 92–93
Code of Professional Conduct, 177–178
Guidelines Relating to Recovered Memories, 179–183

Bass, E., 15–16, 50–53, 56, 93, 96–97
Behavioral basis for psychotherapy, 132–133
Bernardin, Cardinal, 126
Betrayal trauma, 40
Bias, psychotherapist, 99
Bibliotherapy, survivor, 86
Bird v. W.C.W., 20
Bloom, P., 92
Body work, 2, 81–82
Boundary violations, 8, 25, 27, 68–74
and challenges from patients, 73–74
confusion, boundary, 70–72
and contact outside of office, 69
discussion of therapist's problems, 70
and loss of therapist objectivity, 68, 71

Boundary violations (*continued*)
  sexual relations, 69–70
  and therapeutic relationship,
    68–69
Brain, and memory, 32–34
Briere, John, 5
British Psychological Society, statement by, 173–175
Brochures, therapeutic techniques
  described in, 90

California, 21
Canterbury v. Spence, 89
Caudill, O. B., 3, 99
Challenger space shuttle explo-
  sion, 42–43
Checklists, improper use of, 52–53
Children
  lawsuits initiated by, against
    parents, 16–19
  third-party lawsuits with adult,
    20–23
  third-party lawsuits with minor,
    19–20
Clute, S., 96
Cobb v. Grant, 89
Cognitive theories of memory, 34–35
Colorado, 20
Complaints against psychothera-
  pists, 7–10
Concreting, 78
Confrontations, patient-family, 93–
  95, 99
Consent, informed. *See* Informed
  consent
Consultation, 112–116
  patient-specific, 114–116
  routine, 114
  supervision vs., 112–113
Consumer Reports, 126
Cook, Stephen, 126
Cosgrove v. Lawrence, 117
The Courage to Heal (Bass and Da-
  vis), 15–16, 50–51

Davis, L., 15–16, 50–53, 56, 93,
  96–97

Defamation lawsuits, 14, 23
Defining abuse, 51–52
Déjà vu, 33
Denial of abuse, overemphasis on,
  54–56
Detachment of patient, from family, 95
Diagnosis, 47–65
  and asking about past abuse,
    49–50
  checklists, improper use of, 52–
    53
  and clinical judgment, 62–64
  and correlation of self-reported
    child abuse with psychopa-
    thology, 57–60
  of dissociative identity disorder,
    61–62
  and goal of psychotherapy, 56–
    57
  and overemphasis on denial,
    54–56
  and overidentification of past
    abuse, 50–56
  and patient requests, 60–61
  and professional standards, 47–
    48
  and symptoms of abuse, 50, 52,
    54
Discovery rule, 17
Dispute resolution mechanisms,
  alternative, 98–99
Dissociation, 40
Dissociative identity disorder, 61–
  62, 118
Distorted memories, patient signals suggesting, 151
Documentation, 107–112
  with complex symptomatology,
    110–111
  precision in, 112, 113
  and release of previous treat-
    ment records, 111–112
  routine, 108–109
  with unproven techniques, 109–
    110

DSM-IV, 118
"Duty to protect" rule, 10

Emory University v. Porubiansky, 117
Emotional incest, 51
Ethical Principles of Psychologists and Code of Conduct, 47–48, 69, 88–89, 94, 121–123
Ethical standards
  alleged violations of, 28
  determining, 29–30
  of institutions, 15
Ethics committees, patient complaints to, 8–10

Facilitated communication, 27–28
False events, recall of, 42
False memories, 37. *See also* Implanted memories
  controversy surrounding, 131
  creation of, 40–41
False memory syndrome, 24
False Memory Syndrome Foundation, 3, 16, 24, 27, 45, 101
Family relationships, psychotherapy and, 92–100
  confrontations, patient-family, 93–95, 99
  detachment of patient from family, 95
  family mediation, use of, 98–99
  and litigation by patients, 96–98
  and risk management, 99–100
First Amendment, 15–16
Flashbacks, 33
FMS Foundation Newsletter, 3, 13, 23–24, 26, 28, 55, 88, 105
Follette, V., 54
Forensic evaluators, psychotherapists as, 100
Former patients, lawsuits by, 23–29
  allegations in, 23–24
  published cases, 25
  recanters' narratives, 26–29

unpublished cases, 25–26
Frederickson, R., 53, 56–57, 94
Frequency of abuse, 1
Freud, Sigmund, 40
Fundamental attribution error, 63–64

Georgia, 117
Goal of psychotherapy, 56–57, 83
Groff, Judge, 19
Groups
  consultation, 114
  overinterpretation of differences between, 64
  survivor, 86–87
Guided imagery, 78–79

Hamanne v. Humenansky, 25, 61, 70
Hammond, D. C., 91–92
Harvey, M. R., 57
Helling v. Carey, 25
Herman, J. L., 57
Hypnosis, 18, 26, 77–78
  with age regression, 80–81
  and informed consent, 91–92
  memories implanted during, 41–42
  use of, by specialists, 13

Iatrogenic memories, 41–46
Identification of past abuse, 49–50
Illinois, 22
Implanted memories, 27, 41–46
  anecdotal evidence of, 41
  and Mental Health Consumers Protection Act, 124–125
  research supporting, 41–43
  social psychological support for, 43–44
  techniques associated with, 2–3
Inaccurate memories, 37
Incest
  emotional, 51
  lost memories of survivors of, 38
Infant amnesia, 101–102

Informed consent, 88–92, 109
  elements of, 89–90
  with hypnosis, 91–92
  in Mental Health Consumers
    Protection Act, 120–121
  sample form, 149
  with unproven techniques, 90–
    92
Interventions, choice of, 74–77
  outcome studies, use of, 75–76
  patient challenges, handling,
    76–77
  and quality control, 75
Interviewing techniques, 49–50
Intrusion advocacy, 71

Jablonski v. United States, 111–112
Johnson v. Johnson, 16
Journaling, 79
Joyce-Couch v. DeSilva, 25
Judgment, clinical, 62–64

Khatian v. Jones, 23, 99

Lawsuits and litigation, 3
  by adult survivors against par-
    ents, 16–19
  defamation suits, 14
  family litigation, 96–98
  malpractice suits, 10–14, 48
  by parents against psychothera-
    pists, 19–29
  third-party lawsuits, 8, 19–23,
    123–124
Legal standing to sue, 21–22
Letter writing, 27
Liability risks, 4–5. *See also* Diag-
    nosis; Lawsuits and litigation
  complaints, 7–10
  and professional standards, 29–
    30
  supervision, 117–118
Libel, 14
Licensing boards, patient com-
    plaints to state, 9, 10
Lie detector tests, 45

Litigation. *See* Lawsuits and litiga-
    tion
Loftus, E., 36
Lost memories, 37–40
  evidence of, 37–38
  frequency of, 39–40
  and lawsuits by adult survivors
    against parents, 17
  mechanisms related to, 40
  of traumatic events, 38

Magnification, 55–56
Malpractice lawsuits, 10–14, 48
  legal requirements of, 10
  proving of harm in, 13–14
  psychotherapist vulnerability in,
    10–11
  respected minority rule in, 12
  and specialists, 12–13
Maltz, W., 50, 51
Mayer, R., 73
McNamara, E., 88
Mediation, family, 98–99
Memory (generally), 31–46
  cognitive vs. trauma-based theo-
    ries of, 34–36
  importance of understanding,
    31–32
  inaccurate memories, 37
  Penfield's concept of, 32–34
  popular misconceptions about,
    32
  preverbal memories, 101
  repressed memories, 3, 17–19
  of traumas, 34–36
Memory of abuse, 1–2
  creation of false memories, 40–
    46
  implanted memories. *See* Im-
    planted memories
  lawsuits arising from, 15–16
  and lawsuits by adult survivors
    against parents, 16–19
  and lawsuits by parents against
    psychotherapists, 19–29
  lost memories, 37–40

and premature interpretation of memory fragments, 80

requests from patients for help in recovering, 60–61

in women, 2

Memory retrieval techniques. *See* Unproven techniques

Mental Health Consumers Protection Act, 3, 119–125, 133

expert testimony limitations in, 124

informed consent as defined in, 120–121

"reckless induction of false memories" provision of, 124–125

scientific treatment requirement of, 122–123

third-party lawsuit provision of, 123–124

MMPI, 13, 26

Montoya v. Bebensee, 20, 117

Multiple personality disorder, 13, 118

Mutual consultation groups, 114

Nash, M., 80–81

New Hampshire, 18–19

Nontraditional treatments. *See* Unproven techniques

Obsessive-compulsive disorder (OCD), 59

Oksana, C., 81

Osheroff v. Chestnut Hill Lodge, 67

Outcome studies, 75–76

Overidentification of past abuse, 50–56

and definitions of abuse, 51–52

and denial by patient, 54–56

and improper use of checklists, 52–53

and unfounded belief in symptoms, 52, 54

Parents

accusations against, 4

lawsuits by, against psychotherapists, 19–29

lawsuits by adult survivors against, 16–19

Patients. *See also* Boundary violations

challenges from, 76–77

complaints against psychotherapists by, 7–10

confrontation with family by, 93–95, 99

detachment of, from family, 95

informed consent of, 88–92

lawsuits by former, 23–29

requests for help from, in recovering memories, 60–61

signals suggesting distorted memories of, 151

Patient-specific consultations, 114–116

Peer consultation groups, 114

Penfield, Wilder, 32–34

Pennsylvania, 22

Polusny, M., 54

Poor, E., 88

Preverbal memories, 101

Private investigators, 27

Professional standards, determining, 29–30

Proving harm, in malpractice lawsuits, 13–14

Psychopathology, child abuse and later, 57–60

Psychotherapists

boundary violations by. *See* Boundary violations

complaints against, 7–10

and family confrontations, 99–100

as forensic evaluators, 100

and identification of past abuse, 49–50

ill feelings of patients toward, 7

Psychotherapists (*continued*)
  lawsuits against. *See under* Lawsuits and litigation
  legal duty of, 19
  objectivity of, 68, 71
  reluctance of, to treat adult survivors of abuse, 2, 4
  skepticism of, 100–105
  statements of, reflecting substandard practices, 147
  third-party lawsuits against, 20–23
Psychotherapy, 67–105. *See also* Diagnosis
  behavioral basis for, 132–133
  bibliotherapy, 86
  and boundaries with patients, 68–74
  and choice of intervention, 74–77
  and concern for family relationships, 92–100
  forensic evaluation vs., 100
  goal of, 56–57, 83
  group therapy, 86–87
  and informed consent, 88–92
  interventions. *See* Interventions, choice of
  negative outcome of, 7
  patient beliefs and expectations about, 76–77
  regulatory mechanisms for, 125–128, 133
  reparenting, 87–88
  role of judgment in, 62–64
  and skepticism, 100–105
  unproven techniques, use of, 77–85, 90–92
  value of, 1
PTSD, 97

Questions, excessively intrusive, 71–72

Ramona v. Ramona, 13, 21, 79, 84
Recanting patients, 24–29
Recordkeeping. *See* Documentation

Recovered memory therapy, judicial acceptance of, 18–19
Reparenting, 3, 13, 67, 87–88
Repressed memory, 3, 17–19
Repression, 40
Respected minority rule, 12
Risk management, 99–100. *See also* Liability risks
  checklist for, 145–146

Satanic ritualistic abuse (SRA), 13, 55–56, 102–105, 118
Schizophrenia, 28, 87
Schools of thought, 12
"Scientifically based treatments," 122–123
Self-help groups, 86–87
Sexual contact, patient-therapist, 69–70
Sexual dysfunction, 62–63
Skepticism of psychotherapists, 100–105
Slander, 14, 23, 99
Social psychology, and support for iatrogenic memories, 43–44
Sodium amytal, 23, 25, 79, 99
Sodium pentothal, 25
Source attribution, 42
Specialists, standard of care for, 12–13
SRA. *See* Satanic ritualistic abuse
Standards of care
  in malpractice suits, 10–11
  for specialists, 12–13
State licensing boards, patient complaints to, 9, 10
State of New Hampshire v. Hungerford, 18–19
State of New Hampshire v. Morahan, 18–19
Statute of limitations, 16–18
Substandard practices, therapist statements reflecting, 147
Sullivan v. Cheshier, 22
Supervision, 112–113, 116–118
Survivor bibliotherapy, 86

Survivor groups, 86–87
Symptoms of abuse, 50, 52, 54
    documenting, 110–111

Talk therapy, 4
Tarasoff v. Regents of the University of California et al., 19, 123
Terr, L., 57, 95
Texas, 20, 23
Therapeutic relationship, 23, 68–69
Third-party lawsuits, 8
    with adult children, 20–23
    and Mental Health Consumers Protection Act, 123–124
    with minor children, 19–20
Tolling, 17–18
Training programs, professional, 128
Trauma
    betrayal, 40
    memory of, 34–36
Trauma-based theories of memory, 34–36
Treatment, choice of. *See* Interventions, choice of
Tuman v. Genesis, 22–23

Unlicensed professionals, increased controls for, 126–128

Unproven techniques, 2–3, 77–85.
    See also Hypnosis
    adequate processing of memories with, 83–84
    age regression, 80–81
    body work, 81–82
    cautions with, 82–85
    documentation with, 109–110
    and established standard of care, 10–11
    guided imagery, 78–79
    informed consent with, 90–92
    journaling, 79
    memory fragments, premature interpretation of, 80
    recovered memory therapy, 18–19
    sodium amytal, 79
    and treatment goals, 83

Wilkinson v. Balsam, 20
Women, memory of abuse in, 2
Working Group on the Investigation of Childhood Memories of Abuse, 45, 57
    final conclusions of, 159–170
Working Group on the Retrieval of Childhood Memories of Abuse, 34

Zipkin v. Freeman, 70

About the Authors

Samuel J. Knapp, EdD, has been the Professional Affairs Officer of the Pennsylvania Psychological Association since 1987. He completed his undergraduate work at Westminster College, received a master's degree from the Indiana University of Pennsylvania, and received a doctorate in counseling from Lehigh University. He is licensed as a psychologist in Pennsylvania. Dr. Knapp has received numerous awards for his advocacy work on behalf of psychologists. He is the author of several books, over 60 professional articles, and is the associate editor of a book series entitled *Innovations in Clinical Practice: A Source Book,* published by Professional Resource Press.

Leon VandeCreek, PhD, is Professor and Dean of the School of Professional Psychology at Wright State University in Dayton, Ohio. He received his undergraduate degree from Calvin College, his master's degree from Bowling Green State University, and his doctorate in clinical psychology from the University of South Dakota. He has earned the Diplomate in Clinical Psychology from the American Board of Professional Psychology, and he is a Fellow of several APA divisions. Dr. VandeCreek has held elected positions with the Pennsylvania Psychological Association (including President) and with the American Psychological Association (e.g., Council of Representatives, Board of Educational Affairs). He is a regular reviewer for *Professional Psychology: Theory and Practice,* and a member of the Editorial Board of *Psychotherapy: Theory, Research, and Practice* (Division 29 journal). He is the Senior Editor of a book series entitled *Innovations in Clinical Practice: A Source Book,* published by Professional Resource Press.